CHILDREN OF
HOPE

"The HIV/AIDS pandemic is the greatest opportunity for the Church to be the Church. It is time for us to be the hands and feet of Jesus to those who need compassion."
— RICK WARREN

CHILDREN OF

HOPE

Be touched. Be inspired. Be changed.

VERNON BREWER
with Noel Brewer Yeatts

BOOKS

PUBLISHED BY WORLD HELP, INC. FOREST, VIRGINIA

ISBN 978-0-9788041-2-1

World Help
1148 Corporate Park Drive
Forest, VA 24551
worldhelp.net

World Help exists to fulfill the Great Commission and the Great Commandment through partnering, training, helping and serving, especially in the unreached areas of the world.

To the 15 million children who have
been orphaned by HIV/AIDS and robbed of their
childhood. May they come to know the One who
will never leave them alone.

Contents

Acknowledgements

I am grateful for all who contributed so tirelessly and with such passion to this book—your dedicated actions are the seeds of hope for children who have been orphaned and impacted by the scourge of AIDS:

To our partners in the trenches of the fight against AIDS in sub-Saharan Africa. You are on the frontlines of our efforts to care for these vulnerable children. Thank you for allowing us to partner with you to help give these hurting children a future of hope.

To my daughter Noel, who shares my passion for these children. I have no words to describe how proud I am of your willing heart, your courage and your determination to make a difference for "the least of these."

To Tom Thompson, Skip Taylor, Ben Moomaw, David Day and the entire World Help team, for your efforts 365 days a year to give help and hope to these children and people in need around the world.

To Philip Mitchell, for capturing such compelling photographs of the Children of Hope.

To my editing team, Shelly Roark, Nancy Horton, Kim

Stewart, Eric Vess and Justin Henderson for helping me to so vividly and accurately give a glimpse into the lives of these AIDS orphans.

To Nikki Hart, Nikki Hogsed and the entire *Children of the World* team for putting faces to our vision and a heartbeat to our mission.

To Jane Nelson for being our eyes and ears and for your passion for the Children of Hope.

To my Executive Assistant Caitlyn Hendrickson for keeping my feet to the task and my life in order.

And especially to my wife Patty. I am forever grateful for your constant love and support.

I am thankful that God is allowing us to be a part of His plan to help children affected by AIDS. He is their true Hope.

Preface

I first came face-to-face with the heartbreaking tragedy of AIDS in 1987. I was on a mission trip to Uganda. The devastation was just beginning. Before then, I had only seen news footage or read about the epidemic that was spreading its death grip across the world.

Since then, however, I have seen the face of AIDS in one form or another throughout much of the global work of World Help. The orphans, the hungry, the poverty-stricken, the war victims—AIDS is both a contributing factor to and a product of many of these situations. So, you may be asking, "Why write a book about AIDS now?" "What more can you do?" "Why focus on the children?"

The answer is I believe NOW is the right time. God has given us the desire and ability right now to make a difference. More than ever before, we can offer hope. This is what World Help is all about. This is what we do.

In recent months, God has placed an overwhelming burden on my heart and in the hearts of every staff member at World Help for the children affected by AIDS—those who have been abandoned and orphaned because of this tragic pandemic.

Not only has He given us the desire, but He has also given us the opportunity. Through many years of working alongside local partners in sub-Saharan Africa, we have developed relationships and contacts with individuals and organizations that allow us to reach the children in greatest need with a practical plan for help and hope.

This book will share the story of the most helpless and innocent victims of AIDS. But it will also share how you can make a difference. It is ultimately a story of hope for the future.

I have co-authored this book with my daughter Noel Brewer Yeatts, who shares my passion and vision to impact AIDS orphans. As World Help's Director of Communications, she has worked closely with these children for many years. Traveling to the forgotten corners of the globe where they live, she has hugged them, listened to them and reached out to help.

Because this account is a combination of our research, experiences and opinions, we have written the book using one voice. Unless Noel's name or mine is noted by a particular story or account, the first person storytelling style is from our combined points of view.

Within the following pages, we have shared our heart, our passion and our calling to help the children whose lives have been devastated by AIDS. Some of the names and details have been altered to protect the identity of the children and their privacy. And because of the far-reaching spread of HIV/AIDS, many of the statistics are constantly changing. We have done our best to provide the most up-to-date information.

It is our sincere hope that with this glimpse into the lives of the "least of these" you will be touched . . . inspired . . . and, most of all, changed. And, in turn, you will help transform the life of a child.

Vernon Brewer

Introduction

A LEGACY OF HOPE

Recently, a family friend was diagnosed with a terminal form of cancer and given only two weeks to live. This young mother of five, suffering in extreme pain, had only 14 days to get her affairs in order, say her goodbyes to family and friends, and pass down years of advice and wisdom to her children—long before it was due.

The news hit our community hard. Everywhere I turned, people, especially women, were evaluating their own lives and mentally putting themselves in that horrible position—only two weeks to live. What would you do? How would you spend your time? Where would you begin?

My dad wrote her a note of encouragement the day he heard the news saying, "The value of your life is not measured by its duration, but by its donation. You have made such a wonderful donation." Powerful words that truly described her life—a life well-lived!

At the same time we heard this tragic news, a friend of mine from church was preparing to undergo surgery—a mastectomy—to hopefully eliminate the cancer found only weeks before. She too was suffering from a disease that struck her much too young.

It had been only a week before that the tragic news of the Virginia Tech massacre impacted our whole nation. On the morning of April 16, 2007, the worst school shooting in U.S. history took place only a little over an hour from our World Help headquarters. Thirty-three people, including the gunman, were left dead . . . 33 sons, daughters, husbands, wives and friends. Living that close to Blacksburg, everyone on our staff had a connection to someone who had been on campus that tragic day. There was no way to make sense of such a senseless act. Thirty-three people were dead for no reason. Most of them young students whose lives had been cut terribly short.

As I lay in bed that night pondering all of this depressing news, I picked up a book I had been wanting to read. It was written by Mark DeMoss— *The Little Red Book of Wisdom*.

I read the first words of the first chapter—a quote from Euripides:

> *"No one can confidently say that they will be living tomorrow."*[1]

Wow—words that aptly fit the news of the day. I read on, clinging to every word, until I reached the closing remarks of the first chapter:

> *"We are all wise to invest life's most precious commodity for the greatest return. When I die, whenever that moment comes, I hope my passing will*

echo the psalmist's saying, 'Teach me to
number my days, that I may present to
you a heart of wisdom.'"[2]

It was all too much for one day. The honesty of those words and the confrontation with my own mortality was more than I could bear. I broke down in tears, and for a few minutes I simply could not pull myself together.

Thoughts were racing through my head. What would I do with only two weeks to live? What would happen to the people I would leave behind—to my family—to my two precious boys? Would I have lived a good enough life? What would I have accomplished? Would I have "numbered my days"? What would my legacy be?

The next day, my dad and I were in the office together working on this book. As we focused on telling the story of the children affected by AIDS, it suddenly hit me.

All the questions that raced through my mind the night before, the doubts, the fears; it all came together.

This is the legacy I want to leave. This is how I want to be remembered. And if I only had two weeks to live, this is how I would want to live it: *Helping the helpless, giving hope to the hopeless.*

What better legacy could I leave my own children? I can't think of any better way to be remembered.

But God was not finished teaching me this lesson.

Just days after I returned from my life-changing trip to Africa, as we were putting the finishing touches on this book, God confronted me yet again with this question.

In an ironic twist, my own husband was told he had cancer—the same form of cancer my dad had suffered from 20 years earlier—Hodgkin's Disease. And even more surprising, they were both the same age when they were diagnosed—38 years old. I was reminded once again to "number my days"—only this time, it hit way too close to home.

Perhaps cancer is the closest thing we have here in the West that helps us relate somewhat to the HIV/AIDS crisis in Africa. Cancer seems to affect our lives and the lives of our loved ones in a similar way. But there is a vast difference. In addition to many forms of cancer being treatable and even curable, we also have access to doctors and hospitals. We have access to medicine and testing. We have insurance and support groups. We have hope!

In the end, my husband's doctors determined he did not have cancer. It was a huge scare but also a powerful lesson and wake-up call.

Stephen Covey said that you should live your life by starting with the end in mind—asking yourself what you want written on your tombstone.[3] This is a hard question for anyone to answer. How do you really sum up your life in a few words and what do you want those words to be?

I certainly cannot speak for anyone else, but if I

died tomorrow, I know what I want written about me. I would want people to say: *Noel was passionate about God, passionate about her family and had true compassion for the world.* I can only hope and pray my life actually lives up to that statement.

As a cancer survivor, my dad has a powerful and inspirational mission statement for his life. "Every day, I try to live my life in such a way that I accomplish at least one thing that will outlive me and last for eternity."

What about you? How do you want to be remembered? What will your legacy be?

I pray that at least part of your legacy will be helping the children around the world affected by HIV/AIDS ... the 15 million children who have been orphaned by AIDS[4] ... the Children of Hope!

Noel Brewer Yeatts

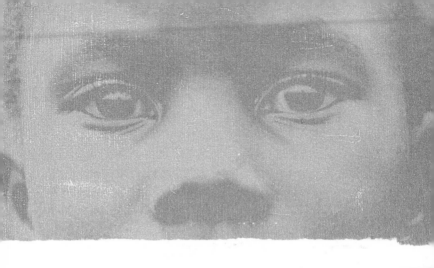

DINDI

trying to understand a world gone mad

Three-year-old Dindi didn't understand why he was always hungry. He was just a small boy who didn't know much about the world.

The watery bowl of porridge he ate once a day never quite made the gnawing pain in his stomach stop. But he knew nothing different. All of his short life had been spent living in a thatched hut with a dirt floor and an animal skin covering the door. He shared the small home with his brother, sister and mother. He had no memories of his father. "The sickness" had taken him before Dindi was born.

Their hut was crammed alongside hundreds of others in a poverty-stricken slum near Zambia's capital city of Lusaka. Dindi didn't understand why screams, shouts and crying noises echoed all hours of the day and night. And the child couldn't know that the sickening stench that hung in the air, along with the cloud of persistent flies, came from raw sewage that ran through the streets. He didn't know the why's of life around him.

But Dindi did know one thing. He knew his mother was sick. And he knew it was bad, very bad. That's why Dindi wouldn't let her out of his sight. The frightened boy lay next to her, wide eyes watching her struggle for every breath.

The toddler had never been farther than a few steps from his mother. He was used to following her everywhere she went or riding in the pouch on her back. She walked for miles in the hot sun to bring back fresh water. She struggled to find peasant work to support her children. She gathered wood and built a fire in the wee hours of the morning. But now she couldn't even get off her bed mat.

Dindi couldn't understand why she kept her eyes closed so much. The little boy tried patting her on the arm and rubbing her forehead. That's what she always did for him when he felt sick. It didn't help. This was bad. Dindi was afraid. He had to stay close, touch her, smell her, to hold on with all his strength!

Dindi refused to leave his mother's side. He

wouldn't budge when his brother Husani asked him to go outside to help gather sticks for a fire and even when his sister Kesia tried to tempt him with his daily bowl of porridge. Kesia, just a child herself, had taken over the cooking and cleaning duties for her mother and was taking care of her brothers as best she could.

They had no food other than what they could beg for. She was grateful for every little bit of grain they could find to make porridge but a little frustrated that Dindi would refuse it. Didn't he know that every meal could be their last? But his stomach was the last thing on Dindi's mind. Nothing was going to pry him away from his mother. If Dindi had taken the time to look, he would have seen the fear and dread in their eyes, too.

He kept his eyes focused on his mother's face. And though he tried to be brave and not whimper, from time to time a lone tear would make its way down Dindi's cheek before he hurriedly brushed it away.

Soon, the exhausted little boy's eyes started to droop. He snuggled closer to his mother's side. He slowly drifted asleep with his tiny hand resting on her thin arm. Those last glimpses of her through heavy eyelids would be the last time Dindi would see his mother alive. As he innocently slept, Dindi joined the 15 million children around the world who are AIDS orphans.[5] His life would never be the same.

It's heartbreaking to think that a child who is little older than a toddler would have to experience the trauma of his mother's death. But for Dindi and others like him, the end of life comes all too soon. There is no escaping the painful reality of their harsh world. Dindi is a child of sub-Saharan Africa—a region of the world ravaged by HIV/AIDS and consumed by death.

When AIDS took their mother, Dindi, his brother and sister were left utterly alone in a situation that was already grim. With no running water and no means for food, the future seemed completely hopeless for the three orphans. They lived in deplorable conditions, surrounded by the stark reality of death.

Try to imagine the devastation of losing not one, but both parents. You're too young to grasp the enormity of the situation. You are left alone with no one to care for you.

In the U.S., government services exist to intervene and place children in a system of care. It may not be perfect, but there is a system. In many regions of Africa, there is no such system. The picture is far more severe. Millions of frightened children like Dindi are left to fend completely for themselves.

Who will care for these children? Who will feed and clothe them? Who will protect them? Who will teach and love them?

Without mercy, HIV/AIDS infects the old and young, claiming the lives of many mothers,

> **"Imagine the entire population of New York, Chicago, and Los Angeles combined infected with HIV, and the magnitude of the catastrophe in Africa is clear."**
>
> Stephanie Nolen, *28: stories of AIDS in africa*[6]

fathers, uncles and aunts, even grandparents. Infected spouses pass it on to their husbands and wives. Mothers infect their unborn children, often without even knowing.

AIDS is the largest public health problem the world has ever faced. It has already surpassed the bubonic plague, which wiped out 25 million people.[7] An estimated 28 million people worldwide have died from HIV/AIDS.[8] Of the 42 million men, women and children still living with HIV/AIDS, 70% are in sub-Saharan Africa.[9]

"If anything, reports out of Africa have become even grimmer, and the continent is beginning to resemble the world of the Black Death even faster than the most pessimistic among us expected. Hospital beds are overflowing, starving children are on the streets, countries that formerly had no data are reporting severe epidemics, and economists are saying

Epidemic - (n.) a disease that attacks great numbers in one place, at one time, and itself travels from place to place: a widespread outbreak.[10]

ZAMBIA AT A GLANCE
Population: 11,668,000
Average Life Expectancy: 38
Population under age 15: 47.1%
Children orphaned by AIDS: 710,000
People infected with AIDS: 870,000[11]

that collapse is imminent in parts of the continent that were beacons of hope."[12]

THE LEAST OF THESE: AIDS ORPHANS

Of all the victims of AIDS, the children suffer most. Whether they are forced into the role of orphan, caregiver, head-of-household or diseased, these youth are robbed of their childhood and their future.

Children suffer unbelievable trauma and emotional distress when one or—as in most cases— both parents are infected with HIV/AIDS. Too often, these boys and girls who are hardly old enough to understand what the disease is must shoulder burdens that would be difficult for even adults. They see and experience more than a child should, learn about things beyond their years, and live with more pain than you and I could ever imagine.

Across Africa, family roles have traditionally been held in high honor. Extended families help care for each other and entire villages help in raising children.

> **"Although the saying, 'It takes a village to raise a child' came from Africa, the village is buckling under the weight of millions of AIDS orphans."**
>
> Charlayne Hunter-Gault, *New News Out of Africa*[13]

But tragically, AIDS is changing this critically shared role. With orphans comprising up to one-third of the population under age 15 in many countries, overwhelmed relatives cannot care for the increasing numbers placed on their doorstep.[14]

"On the continent of Africa, where extended families are legendary, [AIDS orphans] are not wanted. They might contaminate others. The steadily increasing burden of care for dependent children threatens to exhaust capabilities. As a result, children are forced to take responsibility for younger siblings, living as best they can separately from adults. This dilemma is beyond comprehension. Entire communities totter on the brink of chaos."[15]

Grandparents, aunts and uncles already living at poverty level with their own children have nothing left as their household continues to grow. They cannot afford to help the children left to them who are suffering from malnutrition, depression and trauma. Immunizations, healthcare and education are totally out of reach.

These overworked family members are struggling just to survive. Too often, they must make tough decisions to keep their own children fed and clothed.

As a result, the orphaned children end up on their own, living on the streets, or worse.

Owana has already lived a long, hard life for her 12 short years. This native of Uganda's Nansana village watched her father die. The sickness also took the life of a little sister only days after the infant was born. And Owana knows her mother suffers, too, from the illness that has consumed her family and her life—AIDS.

"I have to work with my mother to get food," she said. "I am worried because I have to work hard to take care of the little ones. Before my father died, we still had a rough time because he was a drunkard."

Even though Owana said her life was not easy before, it has never been more difficult than now. For such a young girl, she has a great weight on her shoulders. "My mother and little ones are my family. We continue to suffer harder to get a living."

Eleven-year-old Kabira is even more aware than Owana about what his future holds. He is the oldest child of a single parent stricken with HIV/AIDS.

"My father and brother died of AIDS," he said. "Before my father died, life was not so bad because he used to work and put food on the table and my mom used to stay home and take care of us. Now my daily life is not so easy. I have to work hand-in-hand with my mother. We do peasant work. And I also have to take care of my young brothers just in case my mother dies."

There are countless other boys and girls living like

Every 10 seconds, one person dies of AIDS and another two are infected. A total of 3 million people die each year from AIDS.[16] This staggering number has been compared to 20 fully loaded Boeing 747 airplanes crashing every single day for an entire year.[17]

Owana and Kabira—watching helplessly as one or both of their parents succumb to the illness and die a slow agonizing death. As their parents weaken, young children must assume the role of caregiver.

Death is such a common event for some communities that funerals are held only on weekends to prevent loss of work time. In South Africa, environmentalists predict a disaster because more than 3 million bodies must be buried over the next 10 years. In fact, for the number of deaths in Kwa Zulu Natal Province alone, more than 3,000 football fields will be needed to hold all the dead.[18]

Just outside Port Elizabeth, South Africa, near the township of Motherwell, I saw how overwhelming funerals are on families and villages. A single cemetery we visited holds 300 funerals each weekend. Most of the deaths are attributed to HIV/AIDS. The number seems unbelievable! It still astounds me.

We walked up and down rows of the cemetery and read the tombstones. It was sobering to read the dates and see how many young lives were cut short. Fresh graves were everywhere. The children of AIDS

From Black Death to World Wars

Called "Black Death" because of the black spots it produced on the skin, the bubonic plague erupted in China in the 1330s and spread to western Asia and Europe. It was a swift killer and no Medieval medicine could cure it or even ease the symptoms. Fleas and infected victims caused the disease to spread rapidly. Within five years of the time it was introduced into Europe, 25 million people (one-third of the population) were dead. The total global carnage from Black Death, including China, India, the Middle East and northern Africa, was one-quarter to one-half of the inhabitants of every world region except the Americas.

By the end of 2001, the AIDS epidemic had already surpassed the death totals of Europe from the bubonic plague . . . but not the global carnage. That number will be overtaken by 2010.

More deadly than any war on the planet, HIV/AIDS will soon take more lives than the most devastating world wars. World War I and II together killed 60 million people; Vietnam took 5.1 million lives; and Korea 2.4 million. If this pandemic remains unchecked, researchers predict that AIDS will kill more people than these wars plus the U.S. Civil War, the Bolshevik Revolution, the first Chinese communist war, the Spanish Civil War, the Taiping Rebellion, the Great War in La Plata and the partition of India![19]

live in the shadow of death.

Fifteen million children have been orphaned by AIDS, a number that is expected to increase to 40 million by 2010.[20] Every 14 seconds, a child is orphaned by AIDS in Africa.[21] It's tempting to ignore these numbers and gloss over the fact they represent children's lives that have been devastated.

Today's statistics of orphans are certainly overwhelming, but reports show millions of parents are carrying the disease right now without even realizing it. That means millions more children will become victims and orphans in the next few years. In fact, the United Nations has warned that Africa is in danger of becoming a "continent of orphans" unless we can quickly control the spread of this deadly scourge.[22]

Once AIDS has claimed the lives of their parents, the suffering for orphans has only begun. Rather than having the emotional support to grieve, they must immediately launch into survival mode. They have no idea what the future holds, starting with—"Who will care for me?"

"In a dozen countries, up to a quarter of the nation's children would be orphans. The numbers were completely ridiculous. Twelve million, 14 million, 18 million—how could numbers so high be answers to anything other than, 'How many stars are in the universe?'"[23]

Sometimes the numbers seem so astronomical they simply bounce off our minds and hearts. We are distracted. We are numb. We are disconnected. It's hard to imagine millions of children stripped of their security and left abandoned as orphans—and that's just from AIDS. That doesn't even include the number of orphans from malaria, tuberculosis, war, and famine.[24]

What is so heartbreaking for many of these boys and girls, is that being left alone seems normal. One little girl who was adopted by a family in the U.S. at 5 years old was very good at making friends with other children once she arrived in the States. But she always started a play date or introduced herself by asking the other child, "Do you have a mother?" If she was feeling shy, she would whisper the question to her adopted mother. Most children and adults she met were quite surprised by the question. "Of course she has a mother!" said the grown-ups. But coming from a nation of orphans, the 5-year-old never took it for granted that other children had parents.[25]

This poignant story reminds me that the statistics are not just numbers, they are children—children just like those we love. Children need mothers. They are desperate for fathers. Who will raise the orphans of AIDS? Who will comfort them in the middle of the night from terrors, teach them about their culture, history and religion, and give them values and confidence? Who will share the skills of parenting? No one! AIDS is wiping out an entire generation of parents, teachers, farmers, businessmen, doctors, nurses and more.

ABANDONED AND ALONE

Orphans living with relatives are lowest on the priority list. They get less food, medical care, clothing and schooling than other children in the household. In fact, orphans are more likely to work longer hours, suffer beatings and experience sexual abuse.

Many families in rural areas solve the "orphan problem" by arranging early marriages. Girls are often married off at age 12 or 13.[26] Some children are used as slave labor by their relatives and expected to help make up for the sacrifices of their shelter and care. The children must work hard while living with the fear of an uncertain future.

Thirteen-year-old Ssemboga James of Kibwa, Uganda, knows about working hard. Since his father died, he has lived with a cousin who is a poor farm worker. The young boy's privilege to stay in the home depends on his ability to gather water, wood and help find food. As the only boy in the family, James worries about his sisters. One of his younger sisters, Harriet, died of AIDS. His other sisters live in a different district. "I miss them," he says.

Even those with willing extended families have no guarantee of safety, care and protection. For some children, families are so saturated they have no one to turn to.

Twelve-year-old Calvin and 15-year-old Jackson of Zambia wanted to be soccer stars someday. Their dreams were dashed when their mother died from AIDS and two weeks later, their aunt took them to the bus station. She told the boys she didn't want to take care of them anymore and sent them to Lusaka. She said, "Find a police station and ask for an orphanage."

When the police couldn't help the brothers, they slept in abandoned cars and found food wherever they could. One of the boys said, "Sometimes we are jealous of those who still have parents. It would be nice to have someone who cares about us." In Lusaka alone, 90,000 children, like Calvin and Jackson, call the streets their home.[27]

Motherless and fatherless, children beg for food on the streets, dodging cars and buses in the busy cities. Throughout the countryside, little barefoot girls carry babies in their arms or on their backs as they struggle to exist or find food. Children who are little more than babies themselves are trying to keep their families together by bearing the burden of caring for, clothing and feeding their siblings. It's too much responsibility for a child! How can they survive?

One United Nations Children's Fund (UNICEF) report noted that the "survival strategy" of child-headed households was "eating less."[28]

In addition to the physical battle for survival, these hurting children suffer unbearable emotional problems. They are consumed with grief, anxiety and a fear of the future.

The devastation of AIDS tears families apart, leaving children without stability, love and a sense of

"Before the death of our parents, we were happy. Dad and Mom used to take good care of us. We had a real good life. After their death, we got scattered and started to suffer."

Augustine, 9-year-old AIDS orphan

belonging. "When my father died, my mother left me. I don't know where she is," said 12-year-old Stella. And because of the stigma involved with AIDS, no one explains to children like Stella what's happening. They may not fully understand why their world has been turned upside-down.

Society still has a negative attitude toward those infected. And the children bear the brunt of discrimination as a result. When their parents' illness becomes known, other children are not allowed to play with them. Classmates and teachers ridicule them, leaving them confused and isolated. Because of the stigma, the children are often treated with disrespect and even cruelty.

One Ugandan girl said, "This lady likes mistreating me because my mother is dead. She wants me to sleep with men because I stay in her house. She tells me to be good to them and says this is the only way I can continue to live in her house."[29]

Children who suffer such trauma put up defensive walls that essentially shut down their emotional growth. They don't develop a sense of belonging to a family or community. Many will never develop feelings and emotions such as compassion and don't have the ability for healthy relationships. According to the U.S. Department of Health, Education and Welfare, children who have been stunted emotionally reflect any of the following:

- Abandonment—left to fend for themselves for a long period of time.
- Inadequate supervision or being left alone.
- Involved in activities that are harmful.
- Inadequate medical and dental care.
- Inadequate education.
- Inadequate nutrition.
- Inadequate shelter.[30]

Most children of AIDS suffer from every one of these adverse conditions. We are growing a generation of emotionally handicapped individuals. What will happen to the nations run by adults who never fully developed the feelings of family and compassion— who saw the world sit idly by as their lives were ravaged by disease? If we do not intervene on behalf of these children, future generations will suffer the consequences.

Pandemic — (adj.) Affecting a whole people, epidemic over a wide area - (n.) a pandemic disease.[31]

INNOCENT VICTIMS OF AIDS

The emotional devastation of children is overwhelming, but the most obvious and tragic impact of the AIDS pandemic is revealed in the pain-filled eyes of those who are infected by the deadly disease.

Each of these children was born with the same needs and desires as the children we see every day. And each one is just as susceptible to pain and fear.

More and more women who are of child-bearing age have HIV through no fault of their own. Mothers are passing the disease to their unborn children. These children can be infected before they even enter this world.

Worldwide, 3.2 million children under age 15 have HIV/AIDS.[32]

Before Kambo was born, her mother and father lived in a small, remote village. When her father contracted tuberculosis, the couple was forced to move in search of much-needed medical attention. They could only afford a tiny hut in a slum area just outside the city. Soon, hunger and desperation drove Kambo's mother to join the local sex workers on the road near their home to try and earn a living. Her father died of tuberculosis soon after Kambo was born, leaving her widowed mother to struggle just to survive.

Over time, Kambo's mom became increasingly weak, until she could no longer stand up on her own. Her body was failing. She was diagnosed with HIV/AIDS. Concerned about her young daughter, she took Kambo to a local children's home. She handed her baby over to be raised by strangers. It was all she could do. Within weeks, she was gone. Kambo was an orphan.

What Kambo's mom didn't know was she had already contracted HIV before her baby was born. And she had passed the hated disease on to her daughter. Though she doesn't yet understand the gravity of her condition, the now 9-year-old Kambo must continue the life-and-death struggle.

Sometimes she becomes very ill, weak and bedridden. But when she's up to it, Kambo joins the other children for school, prayers, meals and play. And because the young victim was brought to the home at an early age, it's the only family she knows.

"I have no family, only the children. The home is my family and Jesus is everything for me," Kambo says shyly after much thought.

When asked who is helping her, she says with a smile, "Prayers." She answers that her hope for the future is "only Father Jesus."

Women, girls and adolescents are the most susceptible groups to acquiring HIV/AIDS.

According to UNICEF, in Zimbabwe "100 babies become HIV positive every day; and a child dies every 15 minutes from HIV/AIDS."[33] Can you imagine? In the time it takes you to read this chapter, another child will have died.

CHILDREN OF HOPE

But there are those who will NOT die. There are those you and I can help save! Though ours is a world that at times seems to have gone mad, it's also a place of hope. And it's up to you and me to give that help and hope. As Christ followers, we have a unique challenge.

The question is not really what <u>can</u> we do to change the AIDS pandemic, but rather, do we <u>want to</u> change it?

I have to admit that so far in this global life-and-death crisis, not many from the Church community have shown up. Despite overwhelming statistics and tragic stories of how AIDS has ravaged and destroyed innocent lives, as a whole, American Christians are relatively apathetic.

Studies show that evangelical Christians are the least likely group to help AIDS victims in Africa. World Vision commissioned a Barna Research Group study to determine the willingness of the Christian community to get involved in fighting AIDS. Less than

Less than 3 percent of evangelical Christians said they would help a Christian organization minister to an AIDS orphan.[34]

3 percent of evangelical Christians said they would help a Christian organization minister to an AIDS orphan.[35] Less than 3 percent!

Can these be the same people who profess to follow God, who according to Psalm 68:5 is *"a father to the fatherless, a defender of widows"*? Are these the believers who model their lives after Jesus?

Christ said the ones who inherit His Kingdom would be those who care for others in need. *"For I was hungry and you gave me something to eat, I was thirsty and you gave me something to drink, I was a stranger and you invited me in, I needed clothes and you clothed me, I was sick and you looked after me, I was in prison and you came to visit me . . . whatever you did for one of the least of these brothers of mine, you did for me"* (Matthew 25:35-36, 40). What are "we" the children of God, doing for "them"?

Sadly, many Christians still believe that AIDS is only a disease of homosexuals, prostitutes and drug users. Some think it's a curse from God for sin. We have been slow to respond. Why?

Perhaps because we have forgotten that we serve a God whose Son's life was all about compassion. Jesus did not care how a person became ill, or why they were suffering. He didn't ask if they had done something wrong that caused their suffering He simply reached out, touched them and healed them.

But, many in the Church have chosen to believe that AIDS is God's judgment for sin. Certainly we have sympathy if a person is infected through a blood transfusion, or if a child gets it at birth from their mother. But we have not been able to see or admit that the majority of AIDS cases are from heterosexual activity. In addition, many of the people affected by AIDS are women and children who have done nothing wrong. They have been innocently infected.

Some believe it's strictly an "African" problem. Recently, after I (Vernon) finished speaking at a church in southern California, the pastor stood and said, "Some think the life of a black-skinned, brown-eyed child in Africa is not as important as the life of a white-skinned, blue-eyed child in America. Shame on us!"

Would a child in Zambia or Uganda who has just watched his mother or father die be less devastated than an American child, just because it happens to more of them? What child feels better about having no arms of protection, no loving hands to rely on for food and care just because another child is going through the same thing? Would your child or

"The world's finest doctors, richest donors and strongest governments cannot match the worldwide Church in terms of earthly care and eternal hope ... Our response to HIV/AIDS will be a defining moment in the history of the Church."

Franklin Graham, president of Samaritan's Purse[36]

grandchild be less hungry living on the streets just because others are also digging in trash bins for food?

Or maybe people are just fatigued from images and news stories about the problem and believe the check they wrote once before fulfilled their obligation. The response, especially by believers, has been nowhere close to the widespread proportions of the needs of these desperate children across sub-Saharan Africa.

WHAT WOULD JESUS DO?

Leprosy was the AIDS of Jesus' day. Being the ultimate advocate and example of compassion, Jesus reached out and touched them.

We cannot sit idly by, shake our heads, feel bad and do nothing. We can't simply walk on the other side as if it didn't exist—or maybe if we ignore it, it will go away. No! The Church, more than anyone, has the responsibility to share the hope and love of Jesus Christ.

Bono, the famous rock star and lead singer of the group U2, may be doing more to address the AIDS crisis than any other single person in the world. When speaking at the National Prayer Breakfast in Washington, D.C., Bono asked, "Will American Christians stand by as an entire continent dies?"[37]*

I believe the answer is "no!" It simply *must* be no. Three percent is not good enough. We are better than

*—*You can find a transcript of Bono's speech in Appendix A.*

that. I believe if better informed, American evangelical Christians will step up and do something significant. It is my passion to see the 3 percent increase to 93 percent.

I can't help but hear the sounds of dozens of little voices ringing in my ear. I'm remembering the voices of children from a church and children's center that we support in Gulu, Uganda. As we arrived, these children whose families have been torn apart by poverty, HIV/AIDS and a 20-year civil war, ran to greet us—smiling, laughing and offering handshakes and hugs. Each boy and girl is special and unique. They are children who without our support would not have the opportunity to attend school, a place where they also receive at least one nutritious meal a day. This is a privilege for them and not something they take for granted.

I watched them in their red and green school uniforms play a game that looked somewhat familiar, "Duck, duck, goose" with an African twist. Then the children formed a large circle and began to chant a poem together. I had to listen carefully to understand what they were saying, but once I did, my heart stopped. This is what they called out over and over again:

> *Who is a child?*
> *A child is a person below 18.*
> *What do they need?*
> *Love, care, comfort.*
> *They are young and innocent.*

Give them protection.
They need protection.
How can we turn a deaf ear to such a cry for help?
If we listen to our heart, we can hear them still.
What do they need?
Love, care, comfort.
They are the Children of Hope.

HOPE FACTOR

Dindi's story does not end with his mother's death. When Dindi's mother became very ill, she contacted a nearby children's home—one of our ministry partners. The day she died, workers came to the home to let her know they had three beds open up. They were ready to care for her children. She died knowing that Dindi and his brother and sister would be fed, clothed, educated and taught about the love of Jesus Christ!

There is hope!

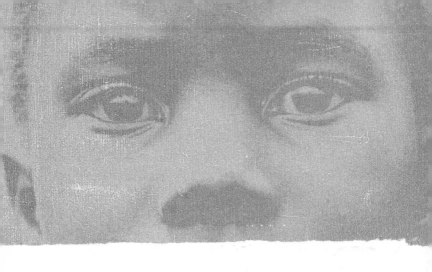

GLADYS

every child is my child

"No one took care of us. Instead, they used us as slaves. I was told to go to the fields to walk before the plowing oxen to give them a straight guide. I would do that from 3 in the morning until about 9 a.m. when I would run to school. At school, some requirements were needed and I had nobody to buy those things for me.

"When I was 9 years I tried to commit suicide because I saw no point in living, but I thought of my younger sister and realized she would be left in this

47

hellish life. I ran home thinking that I could not leave her in this place."

Gladys was just over 6 years old when her mom first abandoned her. The woman left the confused little girl and her sister with an aunt in the Transkei area of South Africa and then disappeared for a year. The child lost much more than her mother during that time. Gladys and her sister were repeatedly raped and molested by family members. As with all children who are sexually abused, the shame and painful memories haunted Gladys for years.

When her mother returned, they began living with cousins. Again the young girls were molested. The mother moved them to live with other distant relatives and once again she disappeared. Gladys started school, but realized that "nobody cared for my welfare, if I went to school or not. But I kept on."

To raise money for books, school supplies and something to wear to school, Gladys gleaned corn from fields. She gathered all the corn left behind during the harvest and sold it to a shop owner.

"No one took care of us. Instead, they used us as slaves."

Gladys, on her childhood

"He would feel pity because I had been carrying a very heavy burden for my age," Gladys said. "Then he would give me the money and a piece of bread. I would say to him, 'No, don't give me money. I want a book, some pencils and material [to make school clothes].' It was very hard. In the time of plowing, I would go and help pick up the wheat gleanings so that I can have money. I had to take care of my younger sister, Alice. I had to make things happen for both of us."

After seven long years, Gladys's mother showed up again and moved them to a boarding school. "It was a dumping place. She just dumped us there. There was no extra money, so she couldn't frequently visit us. But to me, that was heaven. Because I was getting breakfast. I was getting lunch. I was getting dinner. The only thing I had to do was to obey, read my books and study. But when our mother couldn't pay the boarding fees, we were chased away. We went into the neighborhood of this school and asked for accommodation for a short while until she sent money."

Gladys survived her difficult childhood. "God turned my pains into blessings!" Now, she spends her life caring for abandoned and needy children just like herself.

Today, everyone calls her Mama Gladys. The word "Mama" is not used lightly in Africa. It's a word of high esteem. When I sat down and visited with the 57-year-old woman recently in her South African home, she was joyful and gracious but determined to get help for "her children."

She told me approximately 260 babies are abandoned every month in South Africa. They are left at police stations, children's homes, hospitals, fields and trash cans. Mama Gladys is taking in many of these children no one else wants.

"They need education and love. They need clothing. Those are the things we always reach out for. They need moral support," she said. "I know; I was young once. I know; I was destitute also. I was abandoned. Nobody cared for me, so I know how they feel sometimes."

Mama Gladys has 13 children in her home now. As they gather around her, she lovingly points out different ones. "This little boy is a newcomer. His mother just died this year of liver problems. She was an alcoholic. This girl was brought by a young man. She had been staying with an 83-year-old great-grandmom. They heard about us and asked if we could take over because it would be peaceful for the great-grandmom if she dies to leave her in a safe place."

With her children around her, Mama Gladys is the image of Christ's compassion. She cares for the orphaned and abandoned. She is reaching out to the "least of these."

THE RISE OF THE AIDS PANDEMIC

If we look back 25 years to when the disease was first discovered, it's hard to believe how little was known

"Children are the most vulnerable citizens in any society and the greatest of our treasures."

Nelson Mandela, Nobel Peace Prize ceremony, Oslo, Norway, 1993[38]

about how it could be transmitted or treated. The people in Africa named the killer sickness "Slim" because it made a person "too slim until death." They believed it was caused by witchcraft.[39] Others called it "the robber."[40] Now we know the sickness as Acquired Immune Deficiency Syndrome. We know that it's a fatal disease of the immune system caused by infection with the retrovirus HIV. We know that it is contracted through blood or other bodily fluids. And we know there is no cure.

But knowing what we know about it and its transmission, how has it been able to continue to spread so rapidly? Many factors including ignorance, stigma, poverty, war and genocide continue to fuel its advance across the globe.

IGNORANCE

If you live in the country of South Africa, you may be among the one-in-five adults who carry the virus that causes AIDS, but you probably don't know it.[41] Access to HIV testing and healthcare is extremely limited.

Despite almost three decades of information and research in many regions of the world, AIDS is still shrouded in fear, ignorance and superstition.

SOUTH AFRICA AT A GLANCE
Population: 47,432,000
People with AIDS: 5.5 million (1 in 5)
Children orphaned by AIDS: 1.2 million
Total children orphaned by
    all causes: 2.5 million[42]

Many young men continue to believe the myth that having intercourse with a virgin will rid them of the disease. This lie causes the youngest girls (even infants) to be abducted and brutally raped. In a vain attempt to rid one's self of the killer disease, they merely spread it further.

Out of fear, people don't get checked. Therefore, HIV may hide for years, spreading among couples and to their children—growing like a menacing imaginary monster in a child's closet. But this nightmare is real.

STIGMA

One of the greatest obstacles to AIDS prevention and treatment in many countries is the stigma that accompanies this deadly disease. Misconceptions and superstitions keep victims in shame. Those who are infected with AIDS fear prejudice that would isolate them from their families and cause them to lose their jobs. Many fail to get tested for fear of the results. Others who are diagnosed refuse to seek treatment because they don't want anyone to know. HIV

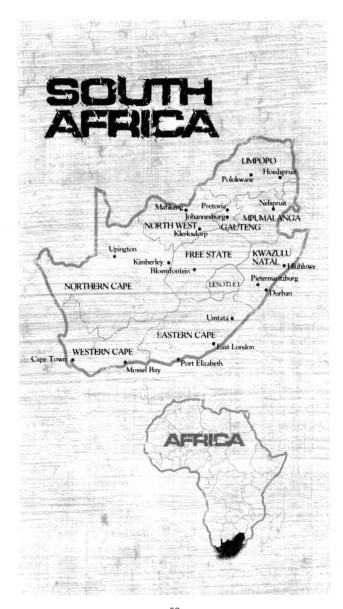

> **"In Uganda, before they knew exactly how to define the disease, one local name for AIDS was, 'The Robber.' After 15 years of direct encounter with this disease . . . I have yet to come up with a better name. HIV/AIDS robs children of parents. It robs families of innocent children. It robs economies of workers. It robs us of friends and co-workers. And it leaves us all the poorer."**
>
> **Dr. Wes Stafford, president of Compassion International[43]**

infection is a secret kept from spouses, families, coworkers and neighbors.

Prisca Mhlolo said, "In our culture, you don't tell. We don't talk, and that is killing our nation." Prisca unknowingly contracted HIV from her philandering husband and passed it to her child. "This confidentiality is killing a lot of people," she said. "Let's look at the woman's side: the husband goes and he is tested, but he doesn't come home and disclose his status. What does that mean? The wife is going to be infected—because he doesn't have guts—she is going to die."[44]

The secrets of a society caught in the iron grip of this pandemic can be deadly. The stigma can hurt as much as the physical pain. Neighbors are ignoring neighbors, friends are talking about each other and family members turn their backs on loved ones.

Rosa, a 37-year-old mother of twins, said her monthly trips to the hospital aroused suspicions among her neighbors. "Always when I walk by I hear them," she said. "They speak loudly enough so I can hear them. They say, 'She is a person of AIDS.'" But Rosa knows the tragic truth. "Today it is me. But tomorrow, it can be them."[45]

Families keep their sick loved ones hidden in a back room to suffer and die alone. In Asian societies, the shame of AIDS is so great that children who have been sold into sexual slavery and infected can never go home. Girls with AIDS can never marry.

Society, families and even people of faith shun AIDS victims. Many Christians still believe that AIDS is a "gay" disease. While HIV/AIDS is many times the result of sinful behavior, in reality all of us are

She was "locked in the house alone!"

"Lisa was left to an alcoholic aunt after her mom abandoned the baby. The aunt rejected her, mistreated her and would leave her alone for long periods of time. One night, neighbors were repairing a car and heard a child screaming. They found the abandoned child locked in the house alone! Another time, the baby was left by the aunt at a business where alcohol is sold. There was no food to give her. She was dying of malnutrition and she was very small. I got Lisa when she was one year and four months. She's been my baby since then. She's growing. She's such a lovely little girl."

—Mama Gladys, South Africa

sinners—*"for all have sinned and fall short of the glory of God"* (Romans 3:23).

But there are many different kinds of stigmatization concerning AIDS in the Church. One woman shared her story at a Prescription for Hope Conference sponsored by Samaritan's Purse in 2002. She confronted her husband for immoral behavior and demanded a clean HIV test before reconciling. He refused and even had the leaders of their church instruct her to "submit to her husband." She refused and they divorced. Her family and church criticized her severely. But within six months, her former husband was dead of AIDS. Because she followed her conscience, despite criticism, their three young children at least have a mother to raise them.[46]

HIV/AIDS isn't the only culprit in the chaos that crushes innocent children around the world. Poverty, violence and war are not only counted among the effects of AIDS, they are its partners, compounding the impact and misery of this fatal evil.

POVERTY

About half the children around the world live below the poverty line.[47] Millions of people across the globe—from India to Asia to sub-Saharan Africa—are

" AIDS is the greatest weapon of mass destruction on earth."

Gen. Colin Powell, former U.S. Secretary of State[48]

already desperate for food and shelter because of the impact of war, drought and famine. And when HIV/AIDS strikes, it takes those who are sexually active—the same people who are the main providers of food, income and care. The orphans who are left have no means to purchase food or find a place to sleep. The children living in unsanitary and poverty-stricken conditions have little resistance against disease and starvation. They don't receive the proper nutrition to grow and to fight sickness.

> **"The children who sleep in the streets, reduced to begging to make a living, are testimony to an unfinished job."**
>
> **Nelson Mandela[49]**

And sadly, many women and children who face starvation because of poverty must do the unthinkable to survive. Mothers sell their bodies for food. Parents sell their young daughters for money to provide for the rest of their family. The sex-slave industry preys on the weak and profits from desperation and poverty. Human life itself is devalued and AIDS runs rampant.

Carol Bellamy, executive director of UNICEF said, "Approximately 1 million children are forced into the commercial sex industry every year and are the most vulnerable to contracting and then spreading HIV/AIDS."[50]

A Continent of Many Nations

Many in the Western world tend to lump the problems and people of the continent of Africa together as if it is one country and one people group. But the story of Africa, while connected, is told from many unique voices. Africa is a land of 53 different countries—each with hundreds of different cultures and languages.

While the entire continent is touched by the HIV/AIDS epidemic, the greatest impact is in sub-Saharan Africa—the area of the African continent which lies south of the Sahara desert. The 42 nations located in this region are among the poorest and most burdened by HIV/AIDS.[51]

WAR AND GENOCIDE

HIV/AIDS, extreme poverty and war are entangled in this great problem facing children across the globe. Rebel fighters and hate-filled murderers have slaughtered men and women during civil war and genocide. Hundreds of thousands of children are orphaned and vulnerable to starvation, abuse and the danger of HIV/AIDS.

The Forgotten Children in Northern Uganda and the orphans of Rwanda's horrific genocide are two prime examples. Just as the children who have been orphaned and impacted by AIDS, these children are in desperate need as well. They live in a world that

SUB-SAHARAN AFRICA

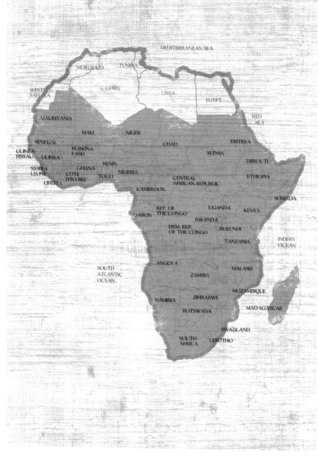

" African countries face a stark choice. If they do not find ways to care for the growing multitudes of AIDS orphans, they could soon find their streets crowded with angry, intoxicated adolescents. Besides being a human tragedy, this could aggravate the continent's already high levels of crime."

Emma Guest, *Children of AIDS: Africa's Orphan Crisis*[52]

makes no sense and seems full of danger and hate.

In light of the famine, poverty, wars and civil violence that plague sub-Saharan Africa, why focus on AIDS? There are so many problems to tackle. What makes AIDS worthy of attention?

A child is orphaned by AIDS and left in the squalor of poverty. But poverty is the reason his mother sold her body for food and contracted HIV. Tortured and abused child soldiers are infected with HIV/AIDS. They grow into hardened rebels who use rape as a weapon of warfare and pass along the deadly disease. The cycle must be broken! AIDS and its impact on the children and the people of sub-Saharan Africa is a crucial place to start.

MIRACLE BABIES

The morning I met Mama Gladys in South Africa, she introduced me to a 3-year-old little girl who liked to be held and didn't mind seeing strangers all around her. I remember her light blue sweater and the sweet way she would lay her head on my shoulder. As Mama Gladys told her story, my heart broke.

"I found Phila-Sande just after her mother died of HIV/AIDS. She was very, very sick and about the size of a 4-month-old, even though she was one year. A young girl visited my home and asked if I knew there was a dying baby somewhere. She said, 'I want to go to school tomorrow. Can I bring that baby to you?' And she brought Phila-Sande.

"With my own eyes, I saw that Phila-Sande was going to die. But with my spiritual eyes, I knew she would make it. She got HIV/AIDS from her mother. Everyone gave up on her. The doctor said, 'Phila-Sande will not make it.' But the miracles of God are amazing.

"Now she is 3. Her progress has been slow. She speaks like a 1-year-old. But her brain is working. She knows. She hears. When we took her back to the doctor, he was surprised. He asked what we were giving her. I told him, 'Love, vitamins and food.' I thank God for Phila-Sande. I call her my miracle baby!"

All of the children that Mama Gladys has helped are miracles. They are miracles because she has reached out to them when no one else cared. Her past has not hindered her. Instead it has motivated her and given her a deep passion and desire to help the hurting children around her.

Mama Gladys told me, "Every child is my child."

If more people truly believed this, we would be living in a very different world.

HOPE FACTOR

Mama Gladys has now returned to the same remote village where she was once sexually abused. She even visited the graves of the relatives who abused her—she has forgiven them. Showing the grace that only comes from God, Mama Gladys now ministers in this village helping needy and orphaned children and providing HIV/AIDS education for the women.

There is hope!

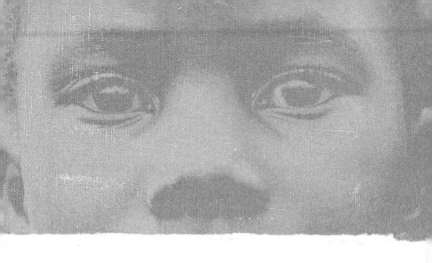

NOZAKE

living with the plague of our times

"There are three [children] in all," she said. "They are all infected. The mother is infected. These kids are suffering. There's nothing at all. They've got no clothing. They've got no food. There's no income at home because the mother is sick. No one is helping them."

Because the traumatized little girl didn't talk much, the kind lady who found Nozake told me her story. As I listened, I almost felt guilty for my life, for my own health and for that of my family.

The little girl named Nozake walked up shyly and never looked me in the eyes. This quiet 10-year-old was one of hundreds of children we met just outside Markman Township, South Africa. All of the women and children who crowded in and around the small, dust-filled concrete compound are affected by AIDS. All are extremely poor, and most have been abandoned.

As we talked with Nozake and the others I thought about how foreign it all seemed to me. These children know nothing but extreme poverty. Every meal is a struggle. School is a privilege not an assumption. Suffering is a daily part of life. Many of them have never lived a day without the effects of AIDS.

I soon found out the reason for Nozake's withdrawn demeanor—this little girl was raped by her mother's boyfriend! The "monster" infected her with HIV. When I heard about the torture this child was forced to endure in her own home, I wanted to put my arm around her and protect her. I knew this child's pain ran deeper than the disease that had invaded her little body. Nozake's spirit was crushed.

In the last year, 3 million people died of AIDS . . . that's about 8,000 per day![53]

My heart was broken. I could only imagine how she must live in fear and shame. How was she supposed to trust anyone ever again? She had not been violated by a stranger, but by someone her mother had allowed into her life.

As I fought back the tears, I hugged Nozake and wished I could take her pain away. I knew I would never forget her.

Nozake and her family are among millions who are living with the pain and impact of AIDS and its daily, never-ending toll.

I remember when AIDS first moved into the global spotlight. What no one could have imagined at the time was it would take only 20 years for AIDS to have a devastating impact on people across the globe. The most obvious impact of this plague is the death count—an estimated 28 million people worldwide have already died—unbelievable! I can hardly fathom the staggering numbers. Deaths in sub-Saharan Africa alone are expected to reach 55 million by 2020.[54]

The numbers cannot adequately describe the horror of AIDS, how it turns healthy bodies into living skeletons. But the devastation is not just about death. It's also the destruction of daily living. AIDS hurts both those who are <u>infected</u> with the disease and those who are <u>affected</u> by the disease. It's about the children who are robbed of their parents, an education, food, shelter and a future, and families who have been torn apart.

The suffering of AIDS is devastating and grotesque. "As I traveled from orphanages in Africa to hospices in Russia to clinics in Thailand, I saw the tortured face of AIDS. It grimaced with the pain of fever and nausea. It gasped with fluid-filled lungs. It wore huge, open sores that emerged from deep in the throat and spread over the lips, neck and torso."[55]

It's not that I didn't have compassion. I just didn't know.

I have a confession to make. A few years ago, I was ignorant about the scope and devastation of HIV/AIDS. I knew people were dying in Africa and we were doing our best to help children in need there. But I'm ashamed to admit that I didn't know all the facts. I didn't know the extent of the devastation HIV/AIDS has caused in Africa in so many ways. It's not that I didn't have compassion. I just didn't know. Now I do. I've seen the pain and suffering firsthand.

I now know that behind every number is a person with a beating heart and desperate soul, just like Nozake. Those of us fortunate to live in a nation that's not completely engulfed by AIDS sometimes have a hard time understanding or relating to those who live so differently than us. After meeting child after child like Nozake, I began to think: "What a different world from mine." But then something happened that changed my mind and heart.

A railroad track ran near the building where we

were meeting. Right in the middle of our visit, we could hear the deep rumble and piercing horn of an approaching train. Boys from across the compound began running to the fence. They lined up with excitement, hooking their fingers into the chain link fence and watching the mighty train rush past. They laughed and gestured with glee as it roared by. Their excitement brought a smile to my face as I remembered the same reaction to trains from my own children and grandchildren. Boys will be boys—no matter if they were born in Lynchburg, Virginia, or Markman Township, South Africa. And boys like trains.

As I watched them, I saw these children for who they were, children just like my own. They are boys and girls like those we love. They feel, they love, they hurt—just like you and me. The only difference is their families and communities are living with a plague that devours all they hold dear.

FAMILIES ON THE EVE OF DESTRUCTION

When I met Agnes, she was almost too shy to speak. She wanted to share her story, but it was just too difficult. Agnes was an orphan before she was even born. Her father died while her mother was still pregnant with her. And when she was only 3, she lost her mother too.

At the time, the cause of her parents' death was irrelevant. Agnes was left alone and that was all that mattered. But years later, the cause would become

Families Torn Apart

After adopting an AIDS orphan from Africa, author Melissa Fay Greene recounts this incredibly touching story of her daughter:

Alone, bringing out the words of the family's end, a child's eyes become bloodshot, the chest fills with sobs. No matter that it is the common experience of this generation to lose Mother, Father, or both, each child has been uniquely hurt.

"I lived in a very small house with my mother," my daughter Helen tells me.

"My mother was very beautiful. She had long, long, long, shiny hair that fell to her waist. We had two things in our house: We had a shelf and we had a baby bed. The bed is too small for my mother, she has to sleep by pulling up her legs. I don't remember when my mother was not sick. I don't really remember my father; sometimes I think I remember him reading a newspaper. My mother taught me to read when I was four … When I was five, I was the one taking care of my mother. If she needed something from the store, I go for her. When she needs juice, she gives me the coin and I go to buy the juice for her. One time I saw at the store little sparkly clips shaped like butterflies for your hair. I wanted those clips very much, but I bought the juice for my mother instead. At home I told my mother about the clips, and she said yes! My mother always said yes. I ran back and I bought the butterfly clips! But one day a taxi came and I think my mother died in the taxi. People took me away and they didn't let me go into the house to get the butterfly clips and I never saw my house again. But why did my mother have to die?"

One day about four months after arriving in Atlanta, Helen collapsed in my arms, suddenly stricken with the memory of her late mother. I held her as she writhed, wailing, "Why she had to die?"

A few moments later, she said between sobs, "I know why she died. She was very sick, and we didn't have the medicine."

"I know," I said. "It's true. I'm sorry."

By then, I was well versed in the AIDS orphan crisis, but it floored me that she captured it with such accuracy, brevity, and grief, more powerfully than any of the thousand pages I had read on the subject.

"I wish I had known you then," I told the child in my arms. "I wish I could have sent her the medicine."

"But we didn't have a phone," she wept, "and I couldn't call you."[56]

very important. Agnes was tested and found to be HIV positive. She is now 14 years old and lives with her elderly grandmother in a very small shack.

Without intervention, HIV/AIDS will sentence the family structure to a slow but certain death. Helpless unskilled women are left to care for their children without a provider. Infected parents must live their remaining days struggling with the thought of leaving their children as orphans. Aging grandparents often in need of care themselves are suddenly faced with the responsibility of raising their children's children.

The sheer number of AIDS orphans is ripping apart the social fabric of the extended family, one of the strongest fibers of African society and culture. Surviving relatives who are willing to care for these children are overwhelmed. This is especially true of grandmothers, who often have lost more than one adult child to the virus and have taken on the responsibility for the grandchildren.

Charlayne Hunger-Gault wrote, "I have sat with many such women around their mud-and-thatch rondavels as the littlest ones played, sometimes naked in the dirt, as the school-age ones sat idly by, their *gogo* [an older relative] unable to afford the fees and uniforms needed for them to go to school."[57]

She also wrote, "In northern Namibia, a government health worker told me the extended family is now so overburdened that people simply turn their heads during the mourning period when the discussion begins about what to do with the children of deceased parents. 'So un-African,' she told me. 'But a sign of the times.'"[58]

It's a job with no rest from the responsibility. Sometimes the dreaded disease is even spread to the caregiver through contaminated blood and other

What AIDS does to the body

- The disease attacks the central nervous system, either causing fingers, hands and feet to go numb or tingle constantly as if pricked by needles.

- Some victims are not even able to close their eyes and mouths.

- A lack of protein destroys the muscles, leaving behind skin and bones.

- HIV weakens the body's defense system. Patients are open to other diseases, painful infections, and life-sapping illnesses.

- Cognitive skills can also be affected. Some suffer from dementia.

- Although antiretroviral drugs can slow the progression of HIV, there is no cure for AIDS.[59]

bodily fluids. Once diagnosed, they know they will soon face their own life-and-death struggle after exhausting their energy on infected loved ones.

I can't begin to imagine what it's like to know that relief will only come with the death of a loved one. This terrible knowledge must only add to their guilt, anger and hopelessness.

Ben Moomaw, a senior staff member of World

Help, travels to Africa multiple times a year. During those visits, he has witnessed the destruction of a family in Uganda. Loziyo and Janet had six children. They lived just across the road from a farm where our partners grow food to help feed the orphans in their care, and where Loziyo occasionally worked.

After becoming very sick, Loziyo learned he had AIDS. He couldn't face the shame and suffering of living with the disease, so he took his own life. He left Janet with six children to raise and a farm full of time-consuming chores with no one to help. His wife had no way to make money, and as their tiny farm began to fail, she had no idea where their next meal would come from.

Finally, she left the four oldest children at the Good Samaritan Children's Home in Kampala. Within a year, she was forced out of her home because the owner wanted to use the land to graze his cattle. Janet left the area looking for a place to live with her two remaining children. Eventually, she returned and now lives in a small hut while a local church raises funds to help her find a permanent home.

Though they are separated from their mother and siblings, the four older children in this family really are the fortunate ones. They are cared for, fed, educated and shown the love of God.

ECONOMIC STABILITY AT RISK

Economic disaster is yet another result of the disease. When the main breadwinners are stricken

" All the best and the brightest are dying—
hard working doctors and nurses, teachers
and professors, civil servants and businessmen,
artists, lawyers, priests—and the core of
society—farmers and miners, lorry drivers
and mechanics, housewives and shop girls,
factory workers and fishermen, policemen
and soldiers—is slipping away, too."

Susan Hunter, *Black Death: AIDS in Africa*[60]

with AIDS, those who are left behind have few
resources and even fewer choices. Houses headed by
women have about a 50 percent greater chance of
being poor than their counterparts.[61]

In sub-Saharan Africa, up to 60 to 70 percent of
large-scale farms have lost a substantial number of
workers due to HIV/AIDS.[62] Such a blow to the
market can drive up food prices and increase the
economic burden of households. As farmers die, they
leave children without the skills or expertise to plant
and grow crops that are critical not only to their own
families but to entire communities.

Eighty percent of Africans depend on small-scale
agriculture for food and income. A study in Zimbabwe
in 1999 showed that AIDS deaths caused maize
production to fall by 61 percent.[63] In Zambia, homes
where a chronically ill person lived planted up to 53
percent less food than other homes.[64]

Because of famine and drought in many regions

hardest hit by AIDS, food supplies are already in jeopardy. Whether confined to the home as victims or caregivers, there is no one to work the fields or bring in outside income.

The growing food crisis has placed 14.4 million people at risk of starvation, in part because 7 million agricultural workers have died of AIDS since 1985.[65] Families must rely on help from government or aid agencies.

Any nation without a strong educational system is a nation without a future.

Not only is AIDS damaging the food chain, it's also holding up production and progress. I'm astounded when I hear that entire workforces are being wiped out—factories have no workers, offices have no skilled labor. Scientists, doctors, nurses, college professors—every career and level of society is touched by AIDS.

EDUCATION ON THE LINE

It's a tragedy to see that education is another casualty of this terrible disease. Because many children must work to help care for sick parents or provide for their remaining siblings, they drop out of school. Others don't have the money to pay costly school fees. For a multitude of reasons, classrooms around the world are being emptied out because of the impact of AIDS.

AIDS is taking a toll on the other side of the school desk as well. HIV/AIDS robs schools of teachers—especially in rural areas where qualified teachers are already scarce. As educators die, nations cannot recruit and train fast enough to keep up with the demand.[66] Without an education, children will not have the skills and knowledge to climb out of poverty. Current statistics show that more than half of adults with no education will live in poverty.[67] Any nation without a strong educational system is a nation without a future.

Imagine what would happen here in the U.S. if school teachers were dying by the hundreds of thousands, schools were closing or turning away students, and parents had no options to provide their children with any kind of formal education.

Ten-year-old Sigwa of Nansana, Uganda, remembers when life was good. "Father worked and took care of us. He put food on the table and we were living in one home," he said. But Sigwa's father and young brother Mukisa died of AIDS. Now Sigwa and one brother live with their aunt. Their living conditions are very poor. His older sister lives in a children's home and his mother "stays in some far place from them."

Despite the impoverished conditions where he lives, Sigwa says he has hope for the future and dreams of becoming a pilot some day. But the only way he can achieve his dream is through an education—a rare privilege for children living under the shadow of AIDS.

" AIDS is not just a medical issue. It is a political, legal, religious, economic, cultural and historic issue."

Dale Hanson Bourke, *The Skeptics Guide to the Global AIDS Crisis*[68]

OVERBURDENED HEALTHCARE SYSTEMS

Available healthcare determines the quality of life and future for the men, women and children infected with AIDS. Antiretroviral drugs (ARVs) can give HIV/AIDS patients the energy and ability to fight debilitating bouts of sickness.

But for many HIV/AIDS victims in developing countries, these life-changing drugs are out of reach. In rural areas, the nearest clinic offering these critical drugs is an hour or more away by car—a nearly impossible trip for the bedridden. And if they could make it, in many places the cost for a year of treatment is far more than they can afford.

As you might imagine, the need for healthcare workers is unbelievable in response to the AIDS crisis. Community health specialists are in high demand. Hospitals, clinics and health systems are overburdened and understaffed. Governments already stretched to the limit on food issues are overwhelmed at the need for medicines, diminishing supplies and care for the rising numbers of AIDS victims and their families.

I was shocked when I heard that one controversial government official claimed a diet of lemon juice, garlic and beets is more effective for treating AIDS than antiretroviral drugs![69] This level of ignorance is unbelievable and unfathomable.

Caring for HIV/AIDS victims includes much more than medications. Patients need help cooking and cleaning when they often feel too tired to even stand. As the disease progresses, they need assistance bathing and dressing. Families suffering from AIDS need emotional support and counseling to deal with fear, anger, despair and the entire range of feelings that come with the sickness.

For caregivers and government agencies, these needs can be insurmountable. And all too often, life can be reduced to financial equations, statistical numbers and budget costs. We must remember that the people who are living with the most horrendous plague the world has ever known are people just like you and me.

If she thinks about it, Esther can still see her father coming home at night to their small village hut in Kibwa, Uganda, from a long day of hard work. She would wait outside and run up to him with a big hug to welcome him home. When he saw her, a big smile always spread across his face as he bent down to grab her up in his arms. Esther's mother would prepare a simple meal and they would sit together, discussing the day's events, laughing and joking. Sounds like a normal evening in any American home.

The 7-year-old was very close to her father. They did chores together and took long walks. Even when she was feeling bad, her father could always make Esther giggle. "Dad loved me so much and took good care of me." But that life soon ended when the young girl's father became very ill. At some point, he had been infected with HIV, and the disease took its toll.

His death left Esther and her mother in severe poverty. Now, the little girl worries far more than a 7-year-old should. She doesn't laugh much anymore. And, more than anything, she misses her father. Esther doesn't want to forget him. His memories are all that she has left of him.

These men, women and children have memories and dreams. Like all of us, they want a home, a family, an education, a career and a hopeful future. But unfortunately, all they can hope for is their next meal, a place to sleep tonight and the strength to live another day. For some, even these basic needs are unattainable.

HOPE FACTOR

"When I grow up ..."

The children of sub-Saharan Africa live with tragedy, but they also live with undefeatable hope. What child doesn't have dreams about what they want to be when they grow up? These children are no exception.

"Someday, I want to be a teacher."—Kezia, age 7

"I want to be a pilot when I grow up."—Sigwa, age 10

"I want to be a pastor."—Masiko, age 9

There is hope!

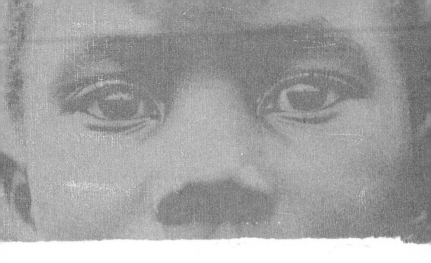

THANDO

the end of poverty

"I grew up in a place where it is not shocking to hear about someone who got killed or hijacked, because it really makes no difference," he said. "I grew up with not just the challenge of living life the way it should be lived, with love and sharing amongst all people, but I grew up with the challenge of having to grow without the guidance of my parents.

"Like many ordinary South Africans, I grew up in the shacks of Cape Town—a place where poor people do bad things to other people to make a living. It is a place where no one wants to live because you see danger everywhere."

Sitting across from me was a grown man. But as I watched Thando share his story, I could see the reflection of a frightened little boy in his eyes. Like so many children in the sub-Saharan region of Africa, Thando grew up under the heavy burden of poverty. Poverty creates a fertile breeding ground for HIV/AIDS by contributing to the hopelessness, desperation, ignorance and superstition that surrounds the killer disease.

As I talked with Thando, I could sense he only wanted to focus on the future. The past was too painful. I carefully asked several questions trying to understand his story. But he answered each one with a positive response. It was only later that Thando was able to communicate his troubled past.

"It's hard to hold onto dreams when you don't have food to eat."

Thando, South Africa

"My people living in these places—called shacks or squatter camps—are living in poverty, and they are always the ones that are abused the most. They suffer the most."

As an orphan, Thando's life was not easy. "No one else was going to provide for me. I had to keep focused," he said. Thando, other orphans and destitute families were crowded together in slums with makeshift housing. In the shacks, Thando lived in squalor and filth. No running water and poor sanitation left many ill. The stench was unbearable and food was scarce. Thando had to beg for barely enough to exist. In addition to his daily struggle for survival, Thando also had to deal with the emotional and physical scars of a terrifying accident.

"The shack I was staying in caught fire and burned to the ground. A baby that was with me in the house died, but I came out alive." The day I met Thando, I noticed he still carries the scars on his face and hands from the consuming fire. The scars of poverty will forever remain with him.

"**P**overty is like living in jail, living under bondage, waiting to be free."[70] And for those living in poverty, an HIV/AIDS diagnosis is a swift death sentence from which there is no escape.

Ezlina Chambukira lives in Malawi where 15 percent of the population is infected with HIV. When her food ran out during the 2002 famine, she began selling all that she owned—a goat, an old umbrella, metal plates and a battered pail. "I have nothing left to sell," said the 36-year-old mother of four. "I was praying, praying for the rains. I was praying for God to give me food." The desperate woman prayed that

More than one-quarter of the developing world's people live in poverty, one-third on incomes of less than $1 a day, and it is in poor countries that HIV/AIDS is the worst.[71]

her children would not join the 14 other people in her village who died from hunger.[72]

Sub-Saharan Africa has the largest proportion of people in poverty—220 million people are living without enough food. In many countries in the subcontinent, close to half of all children are malnourished, leaving them highly susceptible to diseases of all types, including HIV/AIDS.

"In the poor we meet Jesus in His most distressing disguises."

Mother Teresa[73]

Now don't misunderstand this message. Financial success is not the key to happiness and wholeness. Quite the contrary, one study revealed that people living in wealthy countries like the U.S. have the highest rates of depression, suicide and loneliness![74]

THE REAL KILLER

But the grip of poverty on developing countries is choking the life out of many children and their families. These are desperate people without choices. Most of us have no idea the harsh reality of life for Africa's children of poverty.

Malnutrition causes more than 55 percent of child deaths in our world. What's even more shocking is that the earth can actually produce enough food for every man, woman and child to take in 2,720 calories per day—more than any of us really need.[75]

But right now, a child is literally starving to death because her parents have no way to feed her. Orphans are lying listlessly in their own urine, with flies buzzing around their faces because the orphanage has little staff or resources to care for them or provide proper nutrition. I've seen children's homes that are void of everything childlike—no playing, no youthful energy—because poverty strips away joy and innocence, leaving only the desperation for survival.

Families are forced to watch their loved ones wither away because they can't get them the proper nutrition or medical attention. Even America's poor live better than these destitute children and their families. At the very least, our nation's sick can go to emergency rooms and clinics for basic healthcare and help. But sub-Saharan Africa has at least 24 percent of the global burden of disease and only 3 percent of the world's health workers.[76]

Worldwide, one out of every two children lives in the most desperate poverty conditions.[77]

I believe extreme poverty is the root from which many of the world's greatest killers emerge. The poor can't afford nutrition or healthcare to fight diseases.

Sub-Saharan Africa has at least 24 percent of the global burden of disease and only 3 percent of the world's health workers.[78]

Food and good nutrition are absolutely essential for those fighting infection and disease. Millions are dying because they don't have the resources for even the most basic of human needs.

DISEASES RUN RAMPANT

Bono tells us more than 10 million children's lives will be lost unnecessarily to extreme poverty. He says, "Nearly half will be on the continent of Africa where HIV/AIDS is killing teachers faster than you can train them and where you can witness entire villages in which the children are the parents. All over the world, countless children will die as a result of mosquito bites, dirty water and diarrhea."[79]

Mosquitos and diarrhea are mere annoyances in our own lives. But to the children of poverty, they are death warrants. Malaria is the number one cause of death for children under age 5 on the continent of Africa.[80] After being bitten from a parasite-infected mosquito, victims will experience fever, shaking, chills, head and muscle aches and fatigue. Some cases progress to nausea, vomiting and diarrhea. If not treated promptly, the parasites will cause kidney failure and seizures. Eventually, infected children will fall into a coma, never to awaken again.

Malaria kills 3,000 children each day and more

than 1 million each year, the majority in sub-Saharan Africa.[81] Yet this disease is preventable and treatable with something as simple as a $5 mosquito net—a cost out of reach for most families.

Children in developing countries are more susceptible to many diseases because their parents have no resources for vaccinations.

"Lack of access to vaccines means that the world loses over 2 million children every year," said H.M. Queen Rania of Jordan who is on the Board of the Global Alliance for Vaccines and Immunization Fund. "We can save them all. These statistics belong to the children of the developing world, the heartbreak belongs to their parents, but the responsibility belongs to us all."[82]

When children do get sick, infections can be fatal because they have no antibiotics. Children are dying from dehydration because they have no simple rehydration formula to combat diarrhea infection.

"If you haven't noticed, people are dying. It's an emergency."

Jeffrey Sachs, *The End of Poverty*[83]

Half a million mothers are dying in childbirth because they can't afford an obstetrician to stop the hemorrhaging when they try to deliver a child in breech. A simple C-section that has become an ordinary procedure in modern medicine is out

> "Layers of insulation separate the rich and the poor from truly encountering one another. There are the obvious layers like picket fences and SUVs, and there are the more subtle ones like charity. Tithes, tax-exempt donations, and short-term mission trips, while they accomplish some good, can also function as outlets that allow us to appease our consciences and still remain a safe distance from the poor."
>
> Shane Claiborne, *The Irresistible Revolution* [84]

of reach.[85] These are the consequences of extreme poverty.

MORE THAN PHYSICAL PROBLEMS

Poverty means loss of freedom, loss of dignity, and loss of control over the fundamental course of your life.

Afram didn't have a chance or a choice. His uncle, who was given custody after Afram's parents both died, sold him into slavery. Who knows if the uncle needed money or just couldn't afford to care for Afram.

The little boy was used as a commodity. His new owner abused him physically and emotionally and eventually abandoned the 8-year-old. A healthcare worker found Afram sleeping on a tire and suffering from malaria. The boy was traumatized.[86]

In Brazil, the poor compare their existence to "living like a dog, because it makes you so hungry you scavenge, so thirsty you foam at the mouth, so needy you will do anything to make a buck, even sell your body in prostitution."[87]

Many women and children are so desperate for food that they are working as sex slaves. What would you do if your children were in pain and so weak they didn't even have the energy to cry? Would you do whatever you must to feed them?

Sex is a major part of the economy for poor women, who "form steady, sometimes clandestine relationships with relatively wealthy men in the hope it will bring them some material benefit, the occasional chicken perhaps, school fees for the children, or favorable deals for a few cabbages ... [Sex is] practically the only currency they have."[88]

"AIDS is a disease which thrives on poverty."

Dr. Patrick Dixon, *The Truth About AIDS*[89]

Poverty is not just about physical suffering. The poor live with a lack of security and high levels of anxiety. They are also victimized, brutalized, and denied rights to services. The children suffer as adults lose their hold on reality and take out their anxiety and stress on the innocent.

WE HAVE A DECISION TO MAKE

What is the world doing about their pain? The problem of poverty doesn't seem to be going away. Rather, on the continent of Africa, the average

Every day, 22,000 people on the planet die [from] poverty.

World Health Organization report, 2001[90]

household consumes 20 percent less than it did 25 years ago. Children are suffering. Children are dying.

The early believers said that if a child starves to death while a Christian has extra food, then he is guilty of murder. One of the fathers of the Church, Basil the Great, wrote in the fourth century: "When someone strips a man of his clothes, we call him a thief. And one who might clothe the naked and does not—should not he be given the same name? The bread in your cupboard belongs to the hungry; the coat in your wardrobe belongs to the naked, the shoes you let rot belong to the barefoot; the money in your vaults belong to the destitute."[91]

We have been commanded to feed the hungry, clothe the naked and shelter the homeless. But our short-term outreaches and campaigns give only temporary relief. Maybe it's time for a revolution. What if we threw out the old models of charity and really began investing in these communities with not only our resources, but with our hearts?

One homeless mother said, "Managing poverty is big business. Ending poverty is revolutionary."[92]

Dr. Martin Luther King Jr. put it this way, "We are called to play the Good Samaritan on life's roadside . . . but one day we must come to see that the whole Jericho road must be transformed so that men and women will not be constantly beaten and robbed. True compassion is more than flinging a coin to a beggar. It comes to see that a system that produces beggars needs to be repaved. We are called to be the Good Samaritan, but after you lift so many people out of the ditch you start to ask, maybe the whole road to Jericho needs to be repaved."[93]

In the 17th century, St. Vincent de Paul said that when he gives bread to the beggars, he gets on his knees and asks forgiveness from them.[94]

The apostle Paul said, *"But God chose the foolish things of the world to shame the wise; God chose the weak things of the world to shame the strong. He chose the lowly things of this world and the despised things— and the things that are not—to nullify the things that are, so that no one may boast before him"* (1 Corinthians 1:27-29).

"Managing poverty is big business. Ending poverty is revolutionary."

The Irresistible Revolution[95]

Children who are suffering from poverty are certainly weak. And if the statistics say anything about their value in the world, they are "lowly" and "despised." When I consider the helpless children who are suffering from hunger, who are dying needlessly, I am ashamed.

Every time I return from Africa, I wonder how I can even begin to explain what I have experienced.

"I was amazed when I first got to this country and I learned how much some churchgoers tithe. Up to 10 percent of the family budget. Well, how does that compare to the federal budget for the entire American family? How much of that goes to the poorest people in the world? Less than 1 percent."

Bono[96]

The sights and smells—the people—how can I begin to describe it? How can I explain a need of this magnitude?

Sometimes, when I talk with someone about World Help and children in need around the world, I see their eyes begin to glaze over. It's too much for them—too depressing. Perhaps they tune out because of a tinge of guilt.

I know the stories of children affected by poverty, war, genocide and HIV/AIDS are heartbreaking and even hard to read. It's difficult for those of us who live in the West to fully understand what these children endure on a daily basis. It's not part of our world.

I heard a story once of a pastor on a mission trip. Toward the end of the mission he said, "I can't wait to get back to the real world." The missionary he was working with kindly turned to him and said, "You are in the real world."

The world we live in is not the "real world." We live in a bubble; a world more like Disneyland. The rest of the world is reality.

Poverty's Stronghold

The poorest 20 percent of the world's population (4.4 billion people in developing countries) share only 1.1 percent of the world's total income. Here is a quick glance at their situation:

- More than 1 billion people are deprived of basic needs
- Three-fifths of those lack basic sanitation
- One-third are without clean water
- One-quarter are without adequate housing
- One-fifth have no access to modern health facilities and schooling
- One-fifth get too little energy and protein
- 2 billion are anemic[97]

But as much as we need to be aware of this, we don't need to just feel guilty. The point is not to feel bad about your $4 latte or the nice house you live in or the car you drive. You shouldn't feel guilty for the blessings you enjoy. The point is to acknowledge that you have been blessed—but blessed for a reason.

Are we doing only what is required to ease our consciences, or are we reaching out with true compassion and a broken heart? I believe the key is not in how much you give away but how much you hold onto. Don't hold onto your heart! Give it away like Jesus did. Invest yourself in their future.

In his speech during the 2006 National Prayer

Breakfast in Washington, D.C., Bono stated that less than 1 percent of the federal budget goes to the poorest people in the world. He asked our government leaders and all of us to consider an additional 1 percent for the poor—just another 1 percent.

"What is 1 percent? One percent is not merely a number on a balance sheet. One percent is the girl in Africa who gets to go to school, thanks to you. One percent is the AIDS patient who gets her medicine, thanks to you. One percent is the African entrepreneur who can start a small family business thanks to you. [. . .] We're asking for an extra 1 percent to change the world, to transform millions of lives," he said. "History, like God, is watching what we do."[98]

Imagine offering more than a single meal or a new pair of shoes. Think what would happen if we gave these poverty-stricken communities hope for tomorrow through education and job training. What could happen if we each committed 1 percent—just 1 percent? Consider the impact if you and I invested in the lives of the children. We can help these communities become self-sustaining and better equipped to handle the incredible difficulties they face every day.

Jesus is not seeking distant acts of charity. It must be personal. It must be thoughtful. And it must be from the heart. Together, we can think outside the box, dig deep and give these children real help and hope.

HOPE FACTOR

One of the lowest points of Thando's life—being caught in a house fire that scarred his body—is also the memory that gives him the most hope and inspiration.

"While I was in that burning shack, I was in real trouble because the whole house was covered with fire. When I got out, people realized that the clothes I was wearing were not burned at all. But I was badly burned inside my clothes. Those who witnessed the incident say it was a miracle that I survived and I agree.

"Because of that, whenever I come across difficulties, I think of that moment and tell myself that God could not have brought me this far and leave me."

Thando said that every time he sees the burn scars on his body, he realizes he was not born by mistake. "There is a purpose for why I was kept alive. I am here for a purpose and I will never let go of that thought!"

Thando is now a successful music artist and wants to let other young people growing up in poverty-stricken conditions know they have a purpose for their lives also. "Let us not undermine the power that we have within us because of our poor backgrounds. It is true that if you believe that you can do something, nothing can stop you! You just have to find your gift or talent and use it not to destroy yourself, but to improve your life and those around you. The answer is in your hands, not anywhere else but in your hands."

There is hope!

To purchase a copy of Thando's CD, *Shadow Proves Sunshine*, visit our website at www.worldhelp.net.

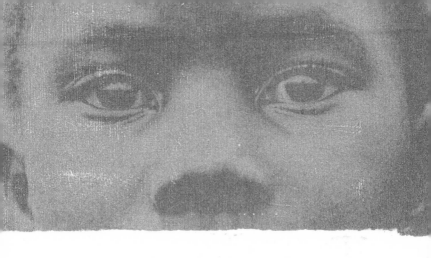

GRACE

victims of war... the forgotten children

As I looked at her, I saw a mere child, shaking and sobbing. Her name is Grace, and her unbelievable story burns in my heart. The memory of that little girl's sad eyes and tear-streaked face will stay with me forever.

When I met Grace in the Northern Ugandan town of Gulu, she was only 13 years old. In her few short years, she had already lived through more pain and terror than many of us endure in our entire lives.

Born in a remote village, Grace lived in a small hut

with her family and grew up like most of the children in the area. She loved her mother and father very much. They were all very happy, until a dark night that would change her life forever.

One moment Grace, who was 11 years old at the time, lay snug in her bed with the rhythmic noises of the village at night lulling her to sleep. In the next instant, the crack of gunfire mixed with yelling and screaming jolted her awake into a living nightmare. Scary, shadowy images violently stormed into her family's hut.

They were members of the dreaded Lord's Resistance Army (LRA)—hordes of cold-blooded murderers. The rebel LRA soldiers murdered her father and severely beat Grace's mother. Then they turned their fury onto the child. They dragged the frightened girl out of the hut and hit her over and over again, telling her they would kill her if she did not do as she was told.

The rebels forced her to carry a weapon and ammunition for their army. She was raped and soon became pregnant by one of the soldiers. Grace had a baby when she was only 12 years old. She was just a child herself! Then Grace was forced to watch while soldiers shot and killed her baby.

What unimaginable pain to watch your child butchered and be helpless to do anything about it! After they killed her baby, Grace tried to escape. She was captured and once again severely beaten—she suffered more than 100 lashes. Despite the dangerous consequences, Grace fled again and finally got away. When she returned home, she found her mother had been stabbed by the rebels and gone insane. She was left with no one to care for her, and no one to comfort her as she struggled with nightmares and memories. There was no one to protect her from being recaptured by the cold-blooded killers of the LRA.

I wept as she told me her story. I prayed with her. Somehow, I wanted to make her life better. I was determined to find some way to give her hope.

Rebel soldiers of the Lord's Resistance Army have raided the countryside at night for years, slaughtering families and looking for children to abduct for child soldiers and slaves. Grace was one of those children. Thousands of children flee their villages each evening to sleep on the streets of nearby cities. They are literally running for their lives.

A young boy named Moses told me, "One night, the rebel soldiers barged into our hut and began beating everyone and dragged us out into the open." He watched as they clubbed his mother and father over and over again. They took Moses and his brother away. He was terrified because he had heard about other children who were kidnapped, but he was relieved that at least he wasn't alone—his brother was with him. That instant of relief quickly disappeared.

UGANDA AT A GLANCE
Population: 28.8 million
Children orphaned by AIDS: 1 million
Children (ages 0-14) with AIDS: 110,000
85% of population lives on under $1 a day[99]

The rebels suddenly stopped by a small stream and turned to the boys. They put a gun to Moses's head. "They told me that if I didn't kill my brother now, they would kill me." Moses could hardly make the words come out of his mouth; he was so ashamed and guilt-ridden.

Moses told me he was crying and kept saying he couldn't do it, but the soldiers were screaming at him and pushing the end of the gun hard into his head. "My brother kept yelling, 'Do it . . . you will live . . . do it!'"

Before he knew what happened, Moses had pulled the trigger and his brother was lying in the dirt. With tears flowing down his distraught young face, Moses continued, "He wasn't moving and there was blood running from his chest."

The LRA's goal is to put so much shame and guilt on these young boys and girls that they feel they can never go home again. And for the most part, it works. Moses was visibly shaken as he recounted his tragic story. I gently told him that God understood and

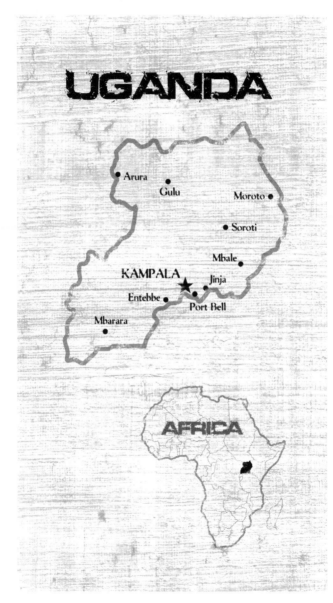

would forgive him. It wasn't his fault. Even more than physical help, children like Moses must learn about the forgiving love of Jesus Christ.

At the height of the rebel attacks, over 40,000 children, some as young as 5 years old, left their villages to take refuge in towns for the night and make the trek back home the next morning.[100] Many walked as far as eight miles each way on their dangerous commute. They had no choice but to flee. These boys and girls were not safe in their own beds!

More than 25,000 children ages 7 to 17 have been abducted from towns and camps since the war started in 1986.[101]

It is impossible to look at the plight of children living in a world plagued by HIV/AIDS, without understanding how war and violence contribute to their pain and suffering. Sub-Saharan Africa is a region of great civil instability. As governments and rebels fight for control, fathers and brothers are murdered, villages burned, women and girls raped and children abducted.

According to reports, nearly 90 percent of LRA fighters in recent years have been enslaved children, kidnapped from their families.[102] By brute force and cruelty, members of the LRA bully children into submission and eventually turn them into killing machines. Once kidnapped, children who refuse to submit or cannot keep up are murdered on the spot. Complaining, expressing sorrow or guilt and not following commands are all grounds for instant death.

As soon as they are abducted, many children are violently forced to kill their own family members.

Any child who is caught trying to escape is brought back to the other young soldiers. These "child soldiers" must then brutally kill the "deserter" with knives, sticks, clubs, rocks, and even bare hands.

Children who manage to escape from this hellish existence are often traumatized beyond description. One young girl tried to tell me a little about her experience but broke down in tears.

"When you stay in the bush," she said, "They call your name, 'You come first . . . you go and kill that person.' You did a lot of things that your life can be destroyed." She could say nothing more.

PEACE TALKS UNDER WAY, BUT PAIN CONTINUES

Peace talks have resumed between the Ugandan government and LRA leaders and a Cessation of Hostilities Agreement was extended to bring a temporary respite from the fighting. Thankfully, because of these talks, the number of children being abducted has drastically dropped. But if violence were to resume, it would be happening again within days. Even though the immediate threat has been suspended, the memories and the fear remain for the children. And the ramifications of this war will

Top 7 Civil Wars in Africa

This list, though hardly exhaustive, provides an overview of some of Africa's major contemporary civil conflicts.

1. Democratic Republic of the Congo

The war in the DRC claimed over 4 million lives, the majority by disease or famine, making it the deadliest conflict since World War II. It involved 20 armed groups from nine countries in what quickly became a scramble to control mineral, diamond and timber wealth in a failing state. Although a truce has been in effect since 2002, most militia groups never disarmed, and the chances for a resumption of violence are high.

2. Sudan

The conflict in the Darfur region of Western Sudan between the Janjaweed, a government-supported Arab militia, and non-Arabs has claimed, by some estimates, 200,000 lives and displaced nearly 2 million people in what many are calling genocide. The Arabs, largely herdsmen, and the non-Arabs, largely farmers, compete over scarce land and water resources. The conflict has direct origins in disputes between the government and southern rebel groups over how to share oil revenues.

3. Uganda

Since 1987, the Lord's Resistance Army has wreaked havoc on the civilian population in northern Uganda. Their purported goal is to create a state based on the Ten Commandments, but most of their activities center around looting villages. Tens of thousands of children have been abducted and used as soldiers or sex slaves, while thousands of civilians have been killed and more than a million displaced. The government has been unable to subdue the LRA which often uses neighboring Sudan to launch attacks.

4. Angola

The conflict in Angola began just after independence in 1974 and formally came to an end in 2002, making it Africa's longest civil war. After independence, the three national groups which overthrew Portuguese rule struggled for control of the country in what became a proxy war for U.S. and Soviet interests.

5. Sierra Leone

From 1991 to 2002, the Revolutionary United Front (RUF) rebel forces fought the government for control over the country and its diamond wealth. Diamonds played a central role in the war, and were used by the RUF to purchase arms and mercenary support from Charles Taylor, then president of Liberia. This conflict is particularly known for the large number of child soldiers and the widespread amputation of civilians.

6. Liberia

A second civil war began in 1999 when a rebel group, Liberians United for Reconciliation and Democracy, emerged in the north. By 2003, a second rebel group, the Movement for Democracy in Liberia, controlled the south, leaving Charles Taylor's government in control of an ever-shrinking portion of the country. Thousands of civilians were killed in the fighting. In the face of mounting international pressure, President Taylor fled to exile in Nigeria.

7. Rwandan Genocide

In 1994 in a period of 100 days, 800,000 Tutsi and moderate Hutu civilians were slaughtered by machete-wielding Hutu militias, also composed primarily of civilians. The genocide in Rwanda has become one of the most notorious conflicts of the 20th century.[103]

continue to impact lives for generations to come.

Children throughout Northern Uganda are struggling for survival. They face the threat of death daily. Some reports estimate that more than 30,000 young boys and girls have died in the conflict.[104] I can't imagine how it must grieve God's heart!

In addition to the abductions and violence of the war, almost 1,000 people die every week in Northern Uganda from malaria, HIV/AIDS and starvation as a direct result of the struggle.[105] Women raped by renegade soldiers and little girls forced into sexual slavery are at high risk of contracting HIV.

The danger of attacks by the LRA displaced 1.7 million people from their homes, forcing them to live in the squalor of Internally Displaced Persons (IDP) camps without adequate food, water or health services.[106]

I have visited many of the IDP camps in Northern Uganda. The living conditions are horrible and

"I come here [to the city each night] to protect myself from the rebels. My parents both died of HIV/AIDS. My father died when I was 9 years old and my mother died a year later. I have five brothers and four sisters. One older brother, who's 15, was abducted by the rebels. He has been gone for two years. He was with two other boys who were killed straight away."

Esther Aloyo, age 13[107]

unsanitary. I have never seen anything else like it in my life. Imagine the worst slum you have ever seen and multiply it times 10. Hundreds of children roam the dirty spaces between huts. Some are clothed in rags; others have no clothes. Many of them are starving. Others are dying from AIDS and other painful diseases.

I met the director of the Palenga IDP Camp in Gulu. He told me this camp houses 17,000 of these displaced people, and of those, 40 percent are HIV positive; and most don't even know it! As I walked through the camp with the director, the sights and smells were unbearable. The huts were so close together you literally had to turn your body sideways to get through.

He led us to the highest point of the camp and from there, the sight was unbelievable: thatch roof huts as far as you could see in every direction.

Walking back, I began asking the director the basic introductory questions—What is your name? Are you married? Do you have any children? I wish I hadn't asked that last question. If I could have taken it back, I would have. But it was too late and his answer still haunts me today.

He explained that four years ago, his son and daughter were abducted by the LRA. His son was only 11 years old at the time. His daughter was 13. They were abducted in the middle of the night at gunpoint. Two months later they found his son who had managed to escape after weeks of torture.

He told me, "They have not found my daughter, yet." That last word "yet" is important because that is how he answered the question—with hope—even after four years. I can't even begin to imagine his anguish.

Because of the ongoing peace talks, many people are starting to leave the camps to return home. But the harsh reality is they have no home left. Entire villages are burned to the ground. Schools are gone; resources have been wiped out. The homeless end up returning to the camps with more hopelessness than ever. At the same time, many are still grieving their losses.

The residents of these squalid camps often suffer from intestinal ailments, meningitis and sexually transmitted diseases. Cholera outbreaks are prevalent.

A PLAN OF HOPE

Through more than two decades of civil war, hundreds of thousands of men, women and children have seen loved ones die. They have experienced the desperation of illness and poverty. But the good news is that through partnership with local churches and Christian organizations in Northern Uganda, World Help has been able to make a difference.

Two years ago, I met with a group of pastors who outlined their plan of hope for the Forgotten Children. They envisioned 10 havens for children called Good Samaritan Children's Centers that would be run by churches in Northern Uganda. I remember

The Reality of War

"I live in a country that is a war zone. Armed soldiers, gunfire and unrest are just a part of everyday life in Northern Uganda.

For 20 years, the government of Uganda and the Lord's Resistance Army have waged violent, bloody warfare in the homes and villages of my people.

On some days, the sights, smells and reality of civil strife can be numbing. But a scene that will never cease to break my heart is that of the "night commuters"—thousands of boys and girls who must flee their homes each evening to sleep in the streets and shelters of nearby towns for safety.

The children of Northern Uganda are the greatest and most precious casualties of this conflict. Their suffering is unbelievable—they have been orphaned, attacked and abused, used as sex slaves, driven from their homes, starved and infected with disease. Yet most of the world has no idea of this great injustice that continues to inflict so much pain on innocent children."

Alex Mitala, World Help partner in Uganda

vividly what one local pastor told me. "It's not that we don't care about these children. We desperately want to help them. But our people are so poor. We just don't have the resources."

I told them World Help would do whatever we could to help. And with God's provision, we did!

Not only have we provided for 10 Good Samaritan Children's Centers, but we've also started a Good Samaritan Vocational School, a place where 220 older

The story of Northern Uganda's Forgotten Children is a success story that is still being told. World Help is giving many of them a life of hope!

children can receive training each year. These centers are in existing church buildings that were previously only used one day a week. We've also provided a sports complex that will facilitate 1,000 traumatized escaped abductees. There are four children's centers in or near the town of Gulu, two in Lira, two in Kitgum and two near Pader. The vocational school is located in Gulu.

Each Good Samaritan Children's Center is also uniquely designed to meet specific needs that are prevalent in the villages and IDP camps near the church. Some are functioning as "day care centers." The younger children come to the centers in the morning and leave late in the afternoon. The centers provide them with three meals a day, an education equivalent to kindergarten and first grade, and the love of Christ.

Other centers provide primary and secondary boarding school education for the older children. There are a number of Christian boarding schools in Northern Uganda that are working with our centers. The pastors regularly check on the progress of the children, and the children stay with the pastors and the church members. This is the wisest approach for children who live in IDP camps.

One of the centers helps teenagers by providing

vocational training programs in fields such as welding, sewing and hair care. This is a good option for many teenagers who have only a seventh-grade education or less. Most are former abductees who have been robbed of an education and cannot qualify for conventional programs.

Literally thousands of former Forgotten Children now have hope for a future. These are children who just a few years ago were making the arduous trek each night into Gulu and other cities for safety—

Breeding Grounds for AIDS, Disease

To provide better protection to the people of the North during violent civil war, the Ugandan government instituted the Internally Displaced Persons (IDP) camps and moved people into them. There are almost 200 camps now, some with populations of just a few hundred, some with thousands of people, and the largest, Pabbo, is home to as many as 63,000.

The IDP camps are composed of mud huts, 10 feet in diameter, with thatched roofs that burn down often. As many as 15 family members are crammed into a single hut. The huts are so close together that it is often hard to walk between them. Water is scarce and toilets are few. Residents are vulnerable to disease from squalor and inhumane conditions. Boredom, anger and hopelessness cause higher instances of rape, promiscuity and alcohol abuse . . . and that places residents at risk of HIV/AIDS.[108]

children who were trying to find enough food to survive in the IDP camps—children who were abducted, brutalized and forced to kill by the LRA.

These children, who were helpless and without hope, are learning to become self-sufficient for the very first time. They are beginning to have hope for the future. And most importantly, they are now learning that Jesus Christ loves and cares about them.

While in Gulu, I met with a most remarkable group of about 20 mothers. They are all HIV positive and have been abandoned by husbands . . . left to raise their children alone.

Hope for Children of War

All of the Good Samaritan Children's Centers:

- Help the neediest children—young children and teenagers in camps or villages who were orphaned when either one or both parents died because of violence or AIDS.
- Show these children the love of Jesus on a consistent basis, week in and week out.
- Provide appropriate educational resources, given the unique needs and situation of each of the children. Education is the key to helping each child escape from hopelessness and poverty.
- Use church resources—the buildings and the members of the church who so desperately want to help.

Journal Entry:

"I had only heard about them, read about them, even viewed a documentary about them—Uganda's Forgotten Children. But now, I was witnessing this experience with my own eyes and ears, and I will truly never be able to forget.

I met Akello. Tears were streaming down her face when she asked me, "What does this mean? Why are they doing this? I don't understand these things." Akello was raped repeatedly at 14 years of age and then given to one of the rebel soldiers as his wife.

I could barely contain my emotions as she told me her horrific story. She told me how she was forced to kill three of her friends from her village before the soldiers took her away.

I am standing with our World Help team on a hill in the middle of a refugee camp that could not have been more than 10 acres, where the local village pastor explained that there were over 3,500 mud huts housing nearly 17,000 people. He took us to visit his modest mud hut church, where hundreds of these refugee boys and girls were waiting for us to come and talk with them. I stood there, in that sweltering building, with my heart breaking, realizing that these families had nothing but the hope that someone would come and bring them help. I tried to encourage them with my words, but they spoke to me through their eyes of pain and desperation. I will never forget!

As we flew over Uganda that day, I prayed, "Lord, please touch me, break my heart, and give me a love and vision for these people to see them as You see them."

Tom Thompson, senior vice president, World Help

> **"It was amazing to see the difference three or four months of someone caring has made in the lives of these kids. I got a chance to meet with the families of some of the children in one of the IDP camps, all of whom were amazed at the positive changes they've seen in their kids after just one term of school. We're making a big difference in a lot of young lives . . . it's incredible what God has given us the privilege of doing together for His Kingdom in Uganda in the last few years."**
>
> Ben Moomaw, vice president of
> International Ministries, World Help

What was so inspirational about these women was their sheer determination. They have not given up on life. They have not lost hope. They are pushing forward together to build a future for their children. All of the women volunteer at a local center that helps to feed needy and orphaned children. They labor over hot fires cooking the food that feeds hundreds of hungry little mouths. They also work a garden to grow fresh vegetables for their family and to sell.

One 36-year-old mother named Kristine shared her story. "I was married when I was 20 and so far, I have five children. The day I found out I had the disease, I thought, 'This is the end of me.' I wanted to commit suicide, because I thought that I would die at any moment anyway."

Kristine said during this dark period in her life she heard about Jesus for the first time. "I accepted Christ as my personal Savior. Since then, my life has changed."

Because the young mother also received vocational training and help from our partners, she said, "Now I am tailoring, baking and making dye. I told them about my sickness and they began to support my family. They sponsored some of my children into the program so that they could have food and schooling. I really appreciate the work of these people. They taught me about the Lord. Now, I know that the Lord I am serving is the One that made the blind to see and the lame to walk. I know that He can touch me."

HOPE FACTOR

On our most recent visit to Northern Uganda, we checked on Grace and Moses. They are both attending boarding school and are excited about their future. We also went to the first graduation ceremony of the Good Samaritan Vocational School we support in Gulu.

This was a very special moment. As I looked onto the crowd of graduates made up of former child soldiers and abductees, I wanted to break down and cry. Many of the girls who were graduating were holding babies and young children—pregnancies that were a result of their captivity in the LRA.

But, I could not cry. Their joy was contagious. We saw these young people celebrating because they now have hope for the future. They were each graduating with a vocation they can use to help support themselves for years to come. What a proud moment and a testament to the power of compassion to transform a life!

There is hope!

JOSIANNE

i did not make myself an orphan

"Almost everyone I knew was gone. I had a family. My mom and dad and relatives, we had a large family. But then my dad was killed and my relatives were killed. Those who lived near us were killed."

Josianne, her mother and her 3-year-old sister were the only ones to escape the brutality. When they returned home, they found it all but destroyed. "Mom couldn't repair our home, so she went into the village to find a man to help. One day, while Mom was home alone, the man raped her. He also infected her with

HIV and made her pregnant," Josianne said.

After Josianne's sister was born, her mother got very sick and eventually died. At 15 years old, Josianne became mother to her two sisters. She feeds and clothes them but struggles to find a way to pay for medication for the youngest. I could sense she had grown up way too fast. At only 24 years of age, she acts much older and has the responsibilities and burdens of a woman twice her age. I asked Josianne if she had any dreams or goals for her life. "My mission is to bring up my young sisters and make sure they grow up and become individuals and establish a family."

Before we left Josianne's modest home in a village filled with child-led households, we stopped to take a quick picture with Josianne and her young sister. The wind was blowing my (Noel) hair and I was having trouble keeping it out of my eyes. Just like a well-experienced mother, Josianne reached up and gently pushed the hair behind my ears. This may sound like a small insignificant detail, but it's something that has stuck with me and reminded me of the burden she bears. Josianne is an orphan—not by choice, and a mother—not by choice.

Josianne and her sisters are among more than one million orphans living in Rwanda as a result of both the 1994 genocide and the growing impact of HIV/AIDS.[109] It is the rule rather than the exception to see older children like Josianne raising younger siblings.

Rwanda, a small country in Central Africa with a population of only 9 million people, has suffered one of the most grotesque genocides in modern history.[110]

" Almost everyone I knew was gone."
Josianne, Rwandan orphan of AIDS and genocide

There is no greater example of the deadly combination of violence, genocide, prejudice, poverty and HIV/AIDS than in Rwanda. How can we ever forget how almost a million men, women and children were massacred in 1994—in just four months?[111] The impact of its destruction still echoes throughout this broken nation.

The rest of the world found out about the travesties of this genocide through news reports and headlines. But Josianne saw it firsthand. She was only 12 years old when the slaughter began.

Between April and July of 1994, the Hutus conducted deliberate and systematic assassinations on the opposing ethnic group of Tutsis and moderate Hutus. From this dark time in history came some of the most horrific stories and brutal images that many of us have ever seen.

The butchers wanted to eliminate the entire Tutsi ethnic group while inflicting as much pain as possible.

RWANDA AT A GLANCE
Population: 9 million
Children orphaned by AIDS and
    genocide: 1 million
Genocide victims: 800,000
Children as heads of households: 101,000
1 in 5 Rwandian children die before age 5[112]

Murderous mobs used machetes, clubs with nails, axes, knives and poles to hack and bludgeon unarmed people. Guns, while available, were rarely used because gunshot deaths were not painful enough.[113]

One Rwandan woman I met told me how she had been captured and her family killed. She was cut so severely that she was left to die on the road. She suffered alone in severe pain for three days until she was found and taken to a hospital. "I know all the people who did this to me. They were our immediate neighbors. I spoke to them, and they gave me time to pray for them before they started cutting me. I prayed for them until I lost consciousness. I know it was the devil that led them to do such an abomination, and I pray the Lord to save their souls from perdition."

All Hutus were encouraged to take part in the massacre or, at the very least, not interfere or offer help to the Tutsis. Teachers turned on their students.

Doctors refused to treat the wounded. Some children were forced to murder their friends or neighbors. Hutu women who had married Tutsis were made to kill their own children. Even the church as a whole turned a blind eye to the tragedy until it was too late. There were some heroic acts of individuals who bravely did what they could to save lives. But noncompliant Hutus who protested or stepped in to help were threatened and then executed—priests, nuns, officials, businessmen—no one was safe.[114]

Hutu leaders were intent on total annihilation. There were to be no survivors. Armed killers searched hospitals, homes, fields, streams, forests and swamps for escapees. Many families fled to local churches for safety. Bloodthirsty mobs threw grenades into the buildings and shot or cut up those who were still alive.

I visited one such church in Ruhanga and heard this horrific story:

The congregation had been a mix of Hutus and Tutsis. When the killings began, women and children fled into the church, while men tried to fight the attackers outside. But church members began fighting each other! The pastor was murdered by an elder because he refused to divide his congregation between Hutus and Tutsis. As he lay dying on the front steps of the church, 4,000 people, mostly women and children, were murdered inside. The men were also killed as they surrounded the building in an effort to protect them.

This terrifying day was all too real for one of our

"Living is War."
Nathan Amooti, World Help partner in Rwanda

partners in Rwanda. As I stood in that church, he told me how his 12-year-old son had come there for safety that day. He narrowly escaped the tragedy by jumping out one of the windows and running to safety.

When the church reopened its doors after the genocide, 600 orphans but no adults attended. Many members of the congregation had died. Those who were left were afraid to go back to the church.

AIDS USED AS A WEAPON IN THE GENOCIDE

Knives, bombs and guns were not the only weapons of the Rwandan genocide. At least 500,000 Tutsi women were systematically raped by men who knew they were HIV positive.[115] This was used as a

1994: Rwanda's Genocide

APRIL: Rwandan president Habyarimana killed in plane explosion

APRIL - JULY: An estimated 800,000 Tutsis and moderate Hutus killed

JULY: Tutsi-led rebel movement RPF captures Rwanda's capital Kigali

JULY: 2 million Hutus flee to Zaire, now the DRC[116]

genocidal weapon to infect as many women as possible and cause suffering and death. Hutu women in mixed marriages were also raped as a punishment.[117]

Years later, the effects of this tragedy are being seen throughout Rwanda. By 2001, an estimated 264,000 children had lost one or both parents to AIDS.[118]

SCARS OF WAR STILL EVIDENT

Everywhere I looked, I could still see the impact of genocide. Children roamed the streets with very little clothing, no place to call home and no one to care for them. I walked through villages where people were starving and children searched dump sites for food. Entire families were reduced to living under pieces of tin that served as their home. The smell in some areas made me sick. These were disease-ravaged human beings who were living lives not much better than animals.

The people of Rwanda are still finding more bodies every day. As prisoners from the genocide are released, they begin to confess where more graves filled with bodies are located.

Just finding a way to bury these bodies is a monumental task. Each coffin contains the remains of about 50 people. They place 200 coffins together (10,000 people) and bury them under a huge stone block. I visited the Kigali Memorial Centre in Rwanda where these coffins are buried. It was overwhelming.

Rwandan Children at Risk

An estimated 1 million orphans and "other vulnerable children" live in Rwanda. These children include:

- 101,000 children heading up an estimated 42,000 households
- 7,000 street children
- 3,500 children living in orphanages
- 1,000 children living in conflict with the law
- 60,000 children living with disabilities
- 120,000 working children
- 300 infants living with their mothers in prison
- children affected by armed conflict (2,500 still in the Congo)[119]

As I walked through the memorial, I saw pictures of children who had been killed during the genocide. Listed were their names, ages, what they liked about school, and what their hobbies and interests were. At the end, it told how they were killed. I could barely read the words—"smashed against a building, macheted in mother's arms, stabbed in eyes and head."[120] It was unimaginable. Babies, toddlers and children coldly slaughtered!

I visited another church compound that was at the center of the genocide. Over 5,000 Rwandans barricaded themselves inside the building, seeking asylum. They were all murdered in one day. Their bodies were locked inside the building and left there as a memorial. When I went in, I saw the bones, skulls, shoes, Bibles, and purses in the same spot where they fell that murderous day. It was beyond description.

You and I can't even begin to fathom the pain and suffering these people must have gone through. Imagine your children clutching at you crying in fear as killers ram the barricaded door. You know eventually they will break through with their

I could barely read the words . . . 'smashed against a building, macheted in mother's arms, stabbed in eyes and head.' It was unimaginable . . . babies, toddlers—children were coldly slaughtered!

"A Day I Will Never Forget!"

"On the outside, the Ruhanga Church seemed just like any of the other churches we had passed by that day in Rwanda except for the fresh paint and a beautiful flower garden. Little did I know what was in store as we walked through the front doors of that particular church building, and what lay ahead for me when I stepped over the threshold. After all, these were doors through which people had walked to hear the Gospel of Jesus Christ preached for many years.

In 1994, the congregation was a mixture of Hutus and

Tutsis. The genocide had just begun to spread across Rwanda. Many of the church's congregation had taken refuge inside the building. Our hosts explained that church members were fighting each other because they were from different tribes. It turned into a bloodbath. When the fighting was finished, over 4,000 women and children were dead.

I walked down the basement stairs and stood among hundreds of coffins. All together, there were 25,000 people buried in that church basement as a memorial to what happened during the genocide. It was hard to comprehend. My mind was in a state of disbelief over what I was hearing and seeing. I was moved to the point of tears and found myself praying for those who experienced this horrendous tragedy. They are still trying to put their lives back together. I immediately thought about the irony of these coffins. To me, they symbolized the millions of orphaned boys and girls who are experiencing another genocide (pandemic)—those who have been infected and affected by HIV/AIDS.

Before leaving, as we stood inside this church that is now a memorial, not a person spoke. Just deafening silence. I thought at that moment, 'Why aren't we crying with a loud voice, a voice of hope for these boys and girls who have been orphaned, who need our immediate help and who need to hear about Jesus? They don't need our silence, our pity, our indifference. They don't need a deaf ear. They need our immediate help. They need hope!'

As we walked out the doors of that church, I asked God to remind me of this great opportunity we all have to be a voice of hope for thousands of children who desperately need our help."

Tom Thompson, senior vice president, World Help

machetes, intent on destroying your children. And you will be helpless to save them. I was standing in the midst of a massive grave. It was a sobering place.

A guard was posted with a machine gun at one of the memorial sites. I asked our partners later in the day why he was there. They explained that if he was not there, the Hutus would come and destroy the church, removing the caskets and bodies. "They don't want the world to know. They want us to forget."

How can anyone forget such suffering and devastation? We must not—we cannot forget! The children depend on us to remember. The acts committed during this genocide were despicable—the rapes, stabbings, and vicious murders. What happened here was inhumane. No one should be slaughtered like cattle right in front of their families.

As I looked at the images of one memorial, a particular quote pierced my heart. "I did not make myself an orphan." The author was listed only as an unknown child affected by the genocide in Rwanda. But the child very well could have been Josianne or any of the other orphans left abandoned.

The ones who are suffering the most are the children. They are innocent. What we do will impact them more than anyone else. It's about the children and the future of Africa, not about the past. We must help the children. And that help must be more than just physical assistance. There are unbelievable emotional scars in the minds and hearts of these

Villages of Children

Our partner, the Anglican Archbishop of Rwanda, Emmanuel Kolini, saw many of his bishops and pastors slaughtered—innocent victims of the 1994 genocide.

He saw tens of thousands of children who suddenly had no adult in their lives. Their parents, aunts, uncles and grandparents were all killed. In family after family, the oldest remaining child was thrust into the role of trying to provide for his or her younger siblings. In just a few short weeks, thousands of "child-headed" households came into existence.

Archbishop Kolini could not just stand by and watch the children struggle, even though the need was massive. He had incredible responsibilities simply trying to reach out to the millions of traumatized adults in his country. But still he managed to organize and build two small children's villages, where almost 50 of these child-headed households are located and where the children have basic shelter and care.

In these villages, the children still maintain their family units. They get to stay together as a family. Additional care, leadership, and oversight is provided by caregivers in the villages, who are the "aunties" for several families. The children have small homes and the opportunity to get an education. Each home has some space for gardens in which they can grow some of their own food. The villages have a leadership committee, which encourages the older children to develop leadership skills. The children even get to elect a chief, usually one of the older boys, along with council members to run the village. Every child has a vote and all can attend the council meetings, which are held on benches under a tree.

suffering boys and girls.

There is a tremendous need for trauma and grief counseling. The genocide took place over 13 years ago and the children who lived through it are now young adults. The memories of such a catastrophic event don't just go away. For many of these children, they are beginning to resurface and manifest themselves in negative ways.

Recently, an American counselor visited Rwanda to help. He tried to relate to young people by sharing his own painful past. The counselor emotionally shared how his own father had abused him as a child. The young people just stared at him in silence. They wondered how something like that could make him so upset. They had witnessed their parents and families being murdered. They were abandoned and left alone. They were struggling simply to survive.

There was no way he could relate to them. He could only offer them love and support. There is no way any of us can relate to their horrific past. But we can offer hope.

Children are the future of Rwanda. According to UNICEF, more than half the population of Rwanda is under 18 years old.[121] They are struggling to pick themselves up out of tragedy and rebuild. But the need is so great in this poor, devastated country. Maybe the response to the genocide of Rwanda was so muted because of the prejudice against the people of Africa. Maybe it is because we've seen too many images of women and children with dirty faces, dust-covered bodies and wearing torn clothes—images of them barefoot, outside small huts with little more than skin and bones. We forget these are people who feel and hurt just like us. God created each of them with gifts and a purpose. They are special to our Creator, and they must become valued by us.

You and I cannot forget or disregard children like Josianne. We must help them pick up the pieces.

What Rwanda's future holds depends on what today holds for its children.

"Children Learn What They Live"
By Dorothy Law Nolte

If children live with criticism, they learn to condemn.

If children live with hostility, they learn to fight.

If children live with fear, they learn to be apprehensive.

If children live with pity, they learn to feel sorry for themselves.

If children live with ridicule, they learn to feel shy.

If children live with jealousy, they learn to feel envy.

If children live with shame, they learn to feel guilty.

If children live with encouragement, they learn confidence.

If children live with tolerance,

they learn patience.

If children live with praise,
they learn appreciation.

If children live with acceptance,
they learn to love.

If children live with approval, they learn
to like themselves.[122]

HOPE FACTOR

Local church leaders of Rwanda said 70-85 percent of the population are illiterate. Our partners there are training men, women and children to read and write through small group discipleship and confirmation classes—using the Bible as their textbook. Children are also discovering the biblical principles of love, forgiveness and righteousness. They are learning to love rather than hate. They are being taught the commands of Jesus—abstinence before marriage and faithfulness during marriage. Because of their newfound faith, they are boldly confronting their culture. They now have hope.

There is hope!

PHOTO JOURNAL

15 million children have been orphaned by AIDS. This number is expected to increase to 40 million by the year 2010.

Mama Gladys is the image of Christ's compassion. Her face shines as she talks about her children: "Every child is my child!"

Vernon Brewer walks through a cemetery near the township of Motherwell in South Africa. Over 300 funerals are held here each weekend. Most of the deaths are attributed to AIDS.

Tom Thompson and 3-year-old Phila-Sande — a "miracle baby!"

Noel Yeatts held Lisa who was locked in a house alone and abandoned when she was only one year old. She is now thriving with Mama Gladys.

138

Children in the compound near the Markman Township in South Africa rush to the fence to see the train pass by.

Martha reminded us that AIDS can happen to anybody. She now reaches out to help children in Zambia who have also been affected by HIV/AIDS.

Worldwide, 3.2 million children under age 15 have HIV/AIDS.

The first Village of Hope is located just outside of Lusaka, Zambia. Our vision is to see hundreds of villages and homes caring for thousands of children all over Africa.

Children living in communities near the Villages of Hope will also benefit from the schools and medical facilities that are provided.

Francis held his mother in his arms as she died from AIDS. With his wife Kimberly and his two children, he now lives in Zambia helping to provide Villages of Hope.

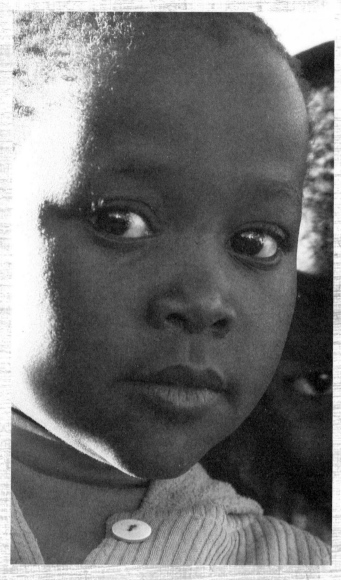

Every 14 seconds, a child is orphaned by AIDS.

Noel and her sister Nikki found Nildo living on the streets of Brazil all alone.

Today, Nildo is a grown man and works in a children's home helping other young people who have been orphaned or abandoned.

There are over 25,000 people buried in the basement of the Ruhanga Church in Rwanda.

Children whose lives have been affected by the genocide in Rwanda captured the heart of Jane Nelson.

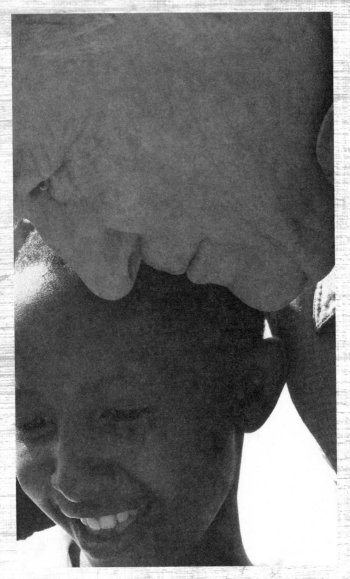

These children are no different than those we love. They deserve and need our compassion.

Aging grandparents who have often lost more than one adult child to the virus now must take on the responsibility of raising their grandchildren.

Noel visited with children from World Help's Child Sponsorship Program in Rwanda.

Josianne is raising her younger HIV-positive sister. She lives in a village full of child-headed households, just struggling to survive.

Over 800,000 people were killed during the genocide in Rwanda, and more bodies are being found every day.

Our partner, the Anglican Archbishop of Rwanda Emmanuel Kolini, has organized and built two small children's villages where almost 50 child-headed households are located. These children now have basic shelter and care.

The IDP camps in Northern Uganda are comprised of mud huts, 10 feet in diameter, with thatched roofs. As many as 15 family members are crammed in a single hut. The huts are so close together that it is often hard to walk between them.

There are 17,000 people living in the Palenga IDP Camp. Of those, 40% are HIV positive.

The director of the Palenga IDP Camp shared that his son and daughter were abducted four years ago by the LRA. His son returned, but his daughter is still missing.

Ben Moomaw was a guest speaker at the very first graduation ceremony of the vocational school in Gulu.

Every graduate was given the tools they need to support themselves in the future, including sewing machines, hair care products and welding equipment.

This graduate is full of joy as she puts her troubled past behind her and looks forward to her new future.

Alex Mitala, one of our partners in Uganda, directs the Good Samaritan Children's Home in Kampala and the Centers in Gulu.

The graduates from the vocational school are all former abductees and child soldiers.

Children at one of the Good Samaritan Children's Centers in Gulu form a circle and chant the poem, "Who is a Child?"

Noel is reunited with one of the children at the Good Samaritan Children's Home in Kampala, Uganda.

This group of HIV-positive mothers in Uganda is helping others in spite of their desperate situation. They all volunteer at a children's center helping to prepare the food that will feed hundreds of hungry children.

Children are the future of Africa. There is hope!

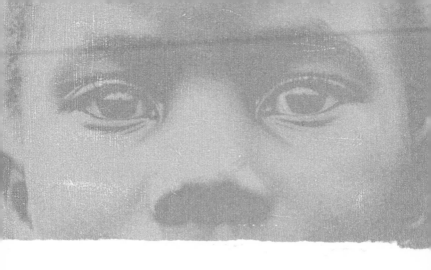

NILDO

compassion in a careless world

Hundreds of thousands of people passed by Nildo every single day. Maybe they didn't notice the little boy wearing nothing but dirty underwear as he slept on a public bench. Maybe they didn't care.

No one showed concern at his deformed, shoeless feet. No one wondered what a wide-eyed 5-year-old was doing wandering around alone. This helpless child was afraid and hungry with no one to protect him, no one to care for him. He was just one of thousands of homeless children wandering the streets of Brazil—

just scenery in their busy lives. But the moment my sister and I (Noel) saw Nildo, he captured our hearts.

You may be wondering what the story of a little boy on the streets of Brazil has to do with AIDS in Africa. Nildo is one of the reasons my father and I are able to write this book. Years ago, God used Nildo to open our hearts to the suffering of children. He was our inspiration. The story of Nildo is the story of why we care. It's also the story of the power of compassion to literally transform a life—whether that of a hungry orphan in Brazil or a dying child in Africa.

It all started when I was 15 years old and traveled to Brazil with my family. My dad led a large group of Liberty University students to distribute Bibles, visit children's homes, and present concerts in public schools, churches, and outdoor plazas. We even built a children's center in one of the worst slums in all of Rio de Janeiro.

A Brazilian pastor told us that over 500,000 people traveled by boat every day to and from work across the bay from Rio. He said, "If you want to catch fish, you must go where the fish are." So we got permission to set up our sound equipment and instruments on the back of a flatbed trailer and we parked it next to the boat docks. Every 30 minutes, more than 20 large ferries with over 5,000 people each pulled into the docks.

As the crowd made its way home from work, we would blast the sound as loud as it would go and perform Christian music in Portuguese. At the end of each concert, my dad gave a simple Gospel presentation. The entire concert and presentation lasted about 45 minutes. We would take a short break and then as more boats began to arrive, we would start all over again. Literally hundreds became Christ followers after each concert.

During one of the concerts, my sister and I were passing out Gospel tracts to the crowd. That is when we saw Nildo—the little boy who would change our lives. He had no shoes, no shirt and no pants. Through an interpreter, we found that he didn't have a father and his mother couldn't afford to take care of him. Nildo was living on the streets, taking care of himself. He had no one. He was all alone.

I remember desperately hunting for my dad to tell him about Nildo. Nildo was obviously hungry so we asked my dad for money to buy him something to eat. The sight of that homeless little boy, with no one to care for him, was just heartbreaking.

My sister said, "Dad, do you see that bench over there? That's where he sleeps and he takes a shower underneath that drain pipe." I asked, "Do you think we could buy him some clothes?" So, my dad sent us off with one of our missionary friends and little Nildo to go shopping.

We went to the local mall to get some lunch and clothes. Nildo ate like he had never eaten before. I still smile when I think about the bright yellow jogging suit he picked out and the new Nike shoes. We took him to the bathroom to clean him up a little before dressing him in his new clothes. As I washed his little feet, I couldn't help but notice they were deformed, apparently from roaming the streets barefooted all of his life. When I slipped on his new Nike's, he kept saying over and over in Portuguese, "Shoes, shoes, shoes," as he pointed to his feet. He was so excited. He had never owned a pair of new shoes!

We could not help them all ... but we could make a difference for one—we could make a difference for Nildo.

We brought him back to the boat docks and he didn't leave our side the whole night. When it came time to go back to the hotel, the police were rushing us to move the trailer and bus. We were blocking traffic and everyone was yelling, so we had to pack up and leave quickly.

It was all happening so fast we didn't even think about what to do with Nildo. But we knew we couldn't take him with us. As we boarded the bus to go, I still remember watching out the window and seeing that little boy in his bright yellow clothes waving goodbye. Everyone on the bus was crying. One of the university students was sitting in the back of our bus. He was a Japanese orphan who had been raised by American parents. He watched little Nildo waving as we drove away and was overcome with emotion and grief. For a few moments, not a word was spoken as his uncontrollable sobbing was heard all the way to the front of the bus.

On our way back to the hotel, my sister and I pleaded with my dad to do something to help Nildo. He made some phone calls and found a Christian foster-care home close by that was willing to take him. The cost was only $400 for an entire year.

Later, when my dad called all of the students together and told them what we could do for Nildo, he took off his hat and passed it around. Of course, it was the end of the trip and all they had left was a little money for snacks and souvenirs. While we were literally "passing the hat," one of the Brazilian pastors who had been helping us leaned over and said, "There are thousands of homeless children on the streets of Brazil. There is no way you can help them all."

I knew he was well-meaning, but I believe it was at that moment God taught me an important lesson, one that has guided my life ever since. That pastor was right, we could not help them all. *But we could make a difference for one.* We could make a difference for Nildo.

When the hat had made its way around the group, we counted the money and there was over $800— enough to provide two years of foster care for Nildo!

We were all so excited as we returned to the boat docks the next day. As soon as we arrived my sister and I started frantically looking for Nildo to give him the wonderful news. But we couldn't find him anywhere. We searched and searched where he had been the day before, but he was not there. Finally, after nearly an hour, we found him several blocks away. He was bloody and bruised, lying in the corner of an abandoned building.

The older street children had beaten the helpless child, taking his clothes and new shoes. All he had left was his dirty pair of torn underwear.

I will never forget the absolute feeling of horror and despair, knowing what little Nildo had been through the night before. We held that broken little boy in our arms and vowed that he would not spend another day on the streets.

We brought Nildo back to the docks and everyone crowded around to comfort him. My sister asked, "Dad, can we buy him some more new clothes?" And, of course he immediately said, "Yes, just don't get bright yellow this time." So off we went again to return with another jogging suit. This time it was gray, with an identical pair of Nike shoes.

But we knew it would take more than new clothes to make a real difference in this precious little boy's life. We asked Nildo if he wanted to get off the streets and live in a Christian children's home where he would receive the love and care he needed. And he immediately said, "Yes."

That night, when it came time to leave, Nildo was on the bus with us!

When we arrived at the hotel, Nildo needed to take a shower and get cleaned up, but he refused to take off his new shoes. Dad tried for 30 minutes to explain that he only had to take them off for five minutes while he was in the shower and then he could put them back on. But Nildo didn't buy it. Finally Dad made a deal with him. He stood right outside the shower, holding Nildo's shoes so he could see them while he showered. As soon as Nildo dried off, he put the shoes right back on. He even slept in them.

The next morning, my dad put his arms around my sister and me and said, "Girls, if you never do another kind deed in your lives, you have done something wonderful for this little boy." God broke our hearts through Nildo.

For the next year, we thought about Nildo often. We kept in touch and received reports that he was doing well in school, attending church, and had even become a believer. The following summer, my dad took another group of students back to Brazil. This time we were unable to join him. We asked him to give Nildo a picture of our family and made him promise to buy him some new shoes.

When my dad arrived in Brazil he gave Nildo a Bible all of us had signed as a keepsake and the framed photo of our family. He said that Nildo hugged it and kissed it and started telling everyone around him in loud Portuguese, "These are my American sisters! They took me off the streets."

I will always remember that little boy on the streets of Brazil. All those years ago, God used Nildo to imprint on my heart His will for my life. He gave me a passion to help the hurting, especially the children around the world. At an early age, He showed me the great desire to not only help meet physical needs but spiritual needs as well. Since then, God has continued to work in my life by giving me the gifts and abilities I need to do the work He has for me.

That day many years ago, on the streets of Brazil, God taught us something very important. He taught us *compassion.*

Most of us consider compassion as simply feeling sorry for someone or having a mild touch of pity. But the Bible defines compassion as much more than that. In Matthew 9:36, when Jesus *"was moved with compassion"* (NKJV), I believe it wasn't just pity that moved Him; it was literally "suffering together with someone."

True compassion is a soul-moving empathy that, at times, seems rare in today's world. Charles Swindoll

"If you have any encouragement from being united with Christ, if any comfort from his love, if any fellowship with the Spirit, if any tenderness and compassion, then make my joy complete by being like-minded, having the same love, being one in spirit and purpose."

Philippians 2:1-2

defines compassion as "showing care in a careless world."[123] In his book, *Come Before Winter,* he shares several compelling examples of a careless world:

Kitty Genovese was brutally attacked as she returned to her apartment late one night. She screamed and shrieked as she fought for her life . . . yelling until she was hoarse . . . for 30 minutes . . . as she was beaten and abused. Thirty-eight people watched the half-hour episode from their windows with rapt fascination. Not one so much as walked over to the telephone and called the police. Kitty died that night as 38 witnesses stared in silence.

Andrew Mormille's experience was similar. Riding on a subway, the 17-year-old youth was quietly minding his own business when he was stabbed repeatedly in the stomach by attackers. Eleven riders watched the stabbing, but none came to assist the young man. Even after the thugs had fled and the train had pulled out of the station, as he lay in a pool of his own blood, not one of the 11 came to his side.

Less dramatic, but equally shocking, was the ordeal of Eleanor Bradley. While shopping on Fifth Avenue in busy

Manhattan, this lady tripped and broke her leg. Dazed, anguished, and in shock, she called out for help. Not for two minutes . . . not for 20 minutes . . . but for 40 minutes, shoppers and business executives, students and merchants, walked around her and stepped over her, completely ignoring her cries. After literally hundreds had passed by, a cab driver finally pulled over, hauled her into his taxi, and took her to a local hospital.

I heard of an experiment a small band of seminary students carried out on fellow members of their class some time ago. I know it is true because I later spoke with one of the men involved. The class was given an assignment on Luke 10:30-37, the familiar account of the Good Samaritan. The assignment was due the next day. Most of the men in that class traveled along the same pathway leading to the classroom the next morning. One of the seminarians in the experiment wore old, torn clothing, disguised himself as though he had been beaten and bruised, and placed himself along the path, clearly in view of all the young students making their way back to class. With their assignments neatly written, carefully documented, and

*tucked under their arms, not one
seminarian so much as paused to come
to his assistance to wipe the catsup off
his neck and chest. Intellectually, the
assignment on love and caring
was completed. But personally? Well,
you decide.*[124]

These examples may seem extreme. But let's face it, we live in a careless world. Nothing could be more needed in our hurting world today than true compassion.

I once had a principal at a Ugandan school remind me of the well-known saying, "We don't care how much you know, until we know how much you care." Our ability to care, our compassion, begins in the heart of Christ. Jesus is the ultimate example of compassion and the greatest advocate for the poor and downtrodden.

LET MY HEART BE BROKEN

At the end of the Korean War, evangelist Billy Graham and Robert Pierce, the founder of World Vision, were faced with the dilemma of thousands of homeless orphaned children. Pierce made a statement that is now famous: "Let my heart be broken with the things that break the heart of God." That's my favorite definition of compassion. Because, apart from the Spirit of God, you and I are not truly compassionate people. We need to continually pray, "Let my heart be broken with the things that break the heart of God." We need to be reminded constantly of Christ's heart of compassion.

When Jesus began his ministry, He announced what was on His heart. In Luke 4:18, He says, *"The Spirit of the Lord is on me to preach good news to the poor."* There are over 2,000 verses in the Bible saying we are to help the poor, including Proverbs 3:27: *"Do not withhold good from those who deserve it, when it is in your power to act,"* and 1 John 3:17: *"If anyone has material possessions and sees his brother in need but has not pity on him, how can the love of God be in him?"*

Nothing could be more needed in our hurting world today than true compassion.

Ten times in the New Testament we find that Jesus was "moved with compassion." All ten times occurred when He was confronted with great human need.

In order to be "one with Christ," in order to have the "same love," we have to know Jesus and what His life was all about.

Jesus spent one-third of His ministry assisting the poor and caring for the sick. In Matthew 9:35 we are told, *"Jesus went through all the towns and villages, teaching in their synagogues, preaching the good news of the kingdom, and healing every disease and sickness."* Caring for the sick, the poor and the downtrodden was a vital part of His ministry.

For our Lord, compassion was a priority not an afterthought. Jesus cared about those in need—not only if He had time, or if the need was big enough, or if He had enough resources. Jesus was *always* "moved with compassion" when confronted with great human need—death, disease, hunger, and the plight of the poor and homeless.

Jesus suffered *with* them. Pity sees and even feels, but compassion touches the need. Compassion requires action. Dr. Paul Brand, in his book, *Fearfully and Wonderfully Made*, says, "Jesus reached out His hand and touched the eyes of the blind, the skin of the person with leprosy and the legs of the cripple ... Jesus knew love usually involved touching."[125]

I NEED TO CARE FOR WHO?

Luke 10 deals with compassion. It's the best known of all the parables of Jesus. In this earthly story with a heavenly meaning, we get a glimpse of three men who all saw a hurting, beaten victim. Only the Samaritan "felt compassion."

The others passed by the man in need, just like the many who passed by Nildo every day. The Samaritan was "moved by" and "suffered with" the victim. He didn't just pass by. He stopped. He touched.

What's even more amazing is Jews despised the Samaritans. They considered Samaritans racially and religiously impure. They would walk around Samaria rather than go the shorter route.

But in spite of all this, the Good Samaritan stopped. He took time out of his busy life and he served someone in need. Someone who despite his race, his occupation, and his location was a neighbor.

So, who are <u>we</u> called to love?

Who is <u>your</u> neighbor?

"Two thousand years after Jesus gave the Church the parable of the Good Samaritan, we are still asking the question, 'Who is my neighbor?' And we're still getting the answer wrong."[126]

I believe Jesus is trying to teach us a very important principle here. "Who is my neighbor?" is not the most important question. The question is, "What kind of neighbor are you?"

Mother Teresa, known for her love and care of lepers, orphans, the destitute and poor in Calcutta always said, "Calcuttas are everywhere if only we have eyes to see. Find your Calcutta."[127]

IT'S ALL ABOUT YOU . . . WELL, NOT REALLY

As Christians, we don't have a choice here. God has called us to be salt and light. He has called us to *"Love your neighbor as yourself"* (Luke 10:27). The Good Samaritan should not be just a parable to remember but an everyday lifestyle to emulate.

Sometimes I think we are hesitant to reach out in love to people because of our own views and prejudices. It's so much easier to help people who deserve help. When it's obvious to us, in all our great knowledge that someone needs and deserves help, we

The Parable of The Good Samaritan

Just then, a religion scholar stood up with a question to test Jesus. "Teacher, what do I need to do to get eternal life?"

He answered, "What's written in God's Law? How do you interpret it?"

He said, "That you love the Lord your God with all your passion and prayer and muscle and intelligence—and that you love your neighbor as well as you do yourself."

"Good answer!" said Jesus. "Do it and you'll live."

Looking for a loophole, he asked, "And just how would you define 'neighbor'?"

Jesus answered by telling a story. "There was once a man traveling from Jerusalem to Jericho. On the way he was attacked by robbers. They took his clothes, beat him up, and went off leaving him half-dead. Luckily, a priest was on his way down the same road, but when he saw him he angled across to the other side. Then a Levite religious man showed up; he also avoided the injured man.

"A Samaritan traveling the road came on him. When he saw the man's condition, his heart went out to him. He gave him first aid, disinfecting and bandaging his wounds. Then he lifted him onto his donkey, led him to an inn, and made him comfortable. In the morning he took out two silver coins and gave them to the innkeeper, saying, 'Take good care of him. If it costs any more, put it on my bill—I'll pay you on my way back.'

"What do you think? Which of the three became a neighbor to the man attacked by robbers?"

"The one who treated him kindly," the religion scholar responded.

Jesus said, "Go and do the same."

Luke 10:25-37, *The Message*

are all over it—like providing meals to new moms or helping someone in our church who is sick. Now, don't get me wrong. We should help in these areas, and I am not saying that it's easy to do the helping—just that it comes easier to initiate the help in such cases.

"Be merciful, just as your father is merciful."
Luke 6:36

But, what about the people who are not as deserving? What about people who have done something wrong to end up in the state they are in—people who have made bad choices, people who have sinned, people who have hurt us? It doesn't come so easily then. But it should.

Rodney Stark, a sociologist and author of *The Rise of Christianity*, cited four traits of the early Christians in the Roman Empire that literally changed their world:

1. The early Christians practiced a high degree of morality without being judgmental. They demonstrated a lifestyle that was an attractive contrast.
2. In a time when infanticide was rampant, when pagans often left girl babies beside streams to be killed by

exposure or wild animals, each morning Christians took these babies into their homes.

3. When plagues hit cities, residents would flee for the relative safety of the mountains. Christians on the other hand stayed to care for the sick and dying. Eventually non-Christian writers began to ask why only Christians showed compassion.

4. In an era in which women were treated merely as property, Christians gave them dignity.

Stark goes on to say, "These actions by God's people literally changed the direction of an empire. Could they not do the same today?"[128]

God has given each of us unique gifts and abilities. And I believe He expects us to use those gifts for His glory. He has paired those talents with passion. Each one of us has a "hot button" that wakes us up inside.

You have been set aside for a special work. Jeremiah 1:5 says: *"Before I formed you in the womb I knew you, before you were born I set you apart . . ."* God has set each one of us apart for a special work.

In Max Lucado's book, *The Cure for the Common Life*, he poses this creative and powerful exercise:

"At a moment before moments existed, the sovereign Star Maker

resolved, 'I will make_____.'
Your name goes in the blank. Then he
continued with, 'And I will make
him/her_____and_____
and_____and_____.'
Fill in those blanks with your
characteristics. Insightful. Clever.
Detail oriented. Restless. And since
you are God's idea, you are a good
idea."[129]

One trap many people fall into is waiting for the
perfect conditions before doing something important
for God. We wait until we are old enough, good
enough or spiritual enough. We wait until we have
more time or more money. But Ecclesiastes 11:4 says,
*"If you wait for perfect conditions, you will never get
anything done" (New Living Translation)*.

Oswald Chambers said, "Christian perfection is
not, and never can be, human perfection . . . It is
a snare to imagine that God wants to make us
perfect specimens of what He can do; God's purpose
is to make us <u>one with Himself</u> . . . God is not
after perfecting me to be a specimen in His
showroom. He is getting me to the place where He
can use me."[130]

We have all been "set apart for a special work,"
and God wants to use you now! According to
1 Corinthians 12:7, *"Each person is given something to
do that shows who God is" (The Message)*.

"If you wait for perfect conditions, you will never get anything done!"

Ecclesiastes 11:4, *New Living Translation*

Isn't that exciting and beautiful? And, isn't that the main point—to show who God is and bring Him glory? It's never about us, but it's always about Him!

TURN YOUR COMPASSION INTO ACTION!

True compassion requires action. "It's not what you believe that counts, it's what you believe enough to do."[131]

James 2:26 tells us, *"Faith without deeds is dead!"* And the same is true with compassion. It's not real unless it moves you to action. Jesus ends the parable of the Good Samaritan by focusing on this very point. *"Which of these three do you think was a neighbor to the man who fell into the hands of robbers?"*

Even though this expert in the law could not bring himself to say the word, "Samaritan," he said, *"The one who had mercy on him"* (Luke 10:37). The Samaritan had true compassion. He was the one who acted and did something about the need.

- Compassion requires answering the question, "Who is my neighbor?"
- Compassion requires you to use the gifts God has given you to make a difference in the lives of others.
- And, true compassion results in action.

In all of Scripture, I never recall Jesus encouraging those who are sick and poor to go find the Church. Instead, He has commanded His followers to seek those in need.[132] You and I have the obligation and the opportunity to reach out with compassion to those in great need. I have never seen a more crucial need than the HIV/AIDS crisis.

But despite the overwhelming statistics, there seems to be a growing apathy toward HIV/AIDS, especially in the Church. I shared these statistics earlier, but they are so shocking they bear repeating: Evangelical Christians are the least likely group to help AIDS victims in Africa, and less than 3 percent said that they would help a Christian organization

Halfway around the world, there is a little boy or girl who is desperately in need of your compassion.

minister to an AIDS orphan![133]

Are these bad people? I doubt it. Does this mean they are not really Christians? No. What it does mean is that many believers may have asked Christ into their heart but don't have *His* heart. It's unbelievable to me, but the statistics seem to show that you can care for Christ without caring for His people. You can listen to what He taught without doing it. You can be thankful for what His compassion did for you without doing the same for others.

Jesus didn't build His Kingdom from the top

down. He built it from the bottom up. He joined those at the bottom—the sick, the poor and the sinners. In fact, He encourages us all to look from the bottom up and become like the "least of these." As the old Franciscan slogan goes, "Preach the Gospel always. And when necessary, use words."[134]

We all know the story in the Bible of Sodom and Gomorrah. And we all know why God destroyed Sodom . . . or do we? Most of us would say it was because of the horrible things they did, especially their immorality. However, in Ezekiel 16:49, we find another reason. It says it was because the people were *"arrogant, overfed and unconcerned; they did not help the poor and needy."*[135] This is so convicting to me!

Jesus used the parable of the Good Samaritan to challenge the religious leaders of His day. But it seems we still need this challenge. Jesus explains that the one who had been the true "neighbor" was the Samaritan, the one who had mercy on the victim. The true neighbor had compassion.

Then He ends the parable with four simple, yet powerful words—*"Go and do likewise."* Imagine the power of that command. We have been commissioned by Christ to help change lives. It has been said that these four words have the power to change the world.[136]

I am sure you will agree that when we stand before God, we want to be able to say, "I did care. I let my heart be broken. I did something. I had compassion."

I realize the numbers and statistics surrounding AIDS are overwhelming. But just like little Nildo, we can make a difference even one life at a time. Look around you. There are people in need everywhere. People with hurts are everywhere. I encourage you to step forward and fulfill God's plan for your life. You have the gifts to reach out to those who are hurting.

Please don't be too busy to notice. Pray that God would allow your heart to be broken with the things that break His heart.

Halfway around the world, there is a child who is in need of your compassion—a child like Nildo. A boy or girl who has been abandoned because of AIDS or poverty. A child who is hungry, frightened and utterly alone. And no one seems to notice.

This lonely child has the same feelings, fears and needs as the children you love. No matter the color of his skin or the type of illness that has ravaged his body, he has a heart, a soul and a mind. He is looking for you. Do you see him now? Please, please don't pass him by. You may be his only hope.

HOPE FACTOR

One Christmas Eve, we were sitting in the family room when the phone rang. It was our missionary friend Donna, who had helped us buy the clothes for Nildo. She said, "Someone wants to talk to you," and she put Nildo on the phone.

He wished us a "Merry Christmas" and a "Happy New Year!" That was about all he could say in English. When Donna came back on the line she told us, "You're not going to believe what I'm about to tell you." She continued, "I am in Rio for Christmas and yesterday I visited the church where we have partnered for the past two summers. The pastor recognized me in the audience and asked me to come to the platform and give a word of greeting.

"While I was speaking, I heard a loud commotion in the balcony and looked up just in time to see a little boy jump from the balcony to the platform. He was yelling in Portuguese 'Auntie, Auntie, Auntie.' I looked down and it was Nildo. He didn't know I was going to be there that day and I didn't expect to see him either. When he saw me he got so excited. And you aren't going to believe what happened next. When I reached down to hug him in front of the entire congregation, he was holding a plastic frame with your family's picture and the Bible you had signed. He must take it with him everywhere he goes."

Today, Nildo has grown into a wonderful young man. I am so proud of him. He has finished school, and he is a committed Christian. He now works in a children's home, helping kids just like him. And we recently heard he is engaged to be married.

When I look at Nildo today, I still see the face of that 5-year-old boy and I can only imagine what his life might have been like had we not met that day.

But God had a plan for his life just like He has a plan for my life and for your life. Nildo is a living reminder that we *can* change the world, one child at a time.

There is hope!

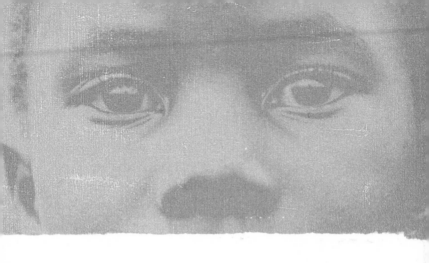

JANE

i am the future of Africa

"I can't remember them. I was only 5 when my mum died and my father died before that. I do feel bad when I hear [other children] calling their mums and dads . . . but I have Grandfather."

Jane welcomed our group into her humble home in Zambia with the grace and hospitality of someone twice her 15 years. She was thrilled to have visitors and to know that someone, *anyone*, would take the time to show they cared. Inside was all the family the little girl had left—her sick grandfather. AIDS had taken both of her parents. Her grandfather is the only person left to care for her. But he, too, has AIDS.

When we walked into the place they call home, it was a shock to our senses. The room was small and very dark. There was a couch and a few other sparse pieces of furniture—very neat and orderly. But the smells were overwhelming. They were the smells of death.

Lying on the couch was a man in the final stages of AIDS. He was recovering from major surgery to remove a tumor from his brain. His head was bandaged, but the gauze didn't look very secure. The sick man was very kind, but he was close to death. He shared how much pain he was in, yet you could still see his faith.

Suddenly, we were compelled to reach out, take him by the hand, and tell him how much we loved him and his granddaughter. I think he was shocked that we would touch him. He looked us in the eyes, weak as he was, and thanked us.

We gathered around this man and prayed for him. We were deeply moved. It was so hard to hear Jane say, "My biggest fear is when Grandfather dies, I will be left alone and I will lose my home. I will have nowhere to go and no one looking after me."

Since her grandfather is too weak to do things on his own, Jane must take care of him. She does the cooking and cleaning. It's a big responsibility for a young child to care for someone so ill.

The heartbreaking fact is that Jane needs care, too.

> ## "She is just a little girl, and yet she has so many burdens to carry."
>
> "The most vivid memory I have of our visit to [Jane's] house was at the end. We were preparing to leave when I saw her by the side of the house. She was leaning up against the wall and crying. Her hands were covering her face. I don't know why she was crying. Perhaps it was all just so emotional. Or, the stress of being filmed and sharing her home and circumstances with total strangers was a bit too much. I'm not too sure, but my heart just went out to her. She is just a little girl and yet she has so many burdens to carry. She is so worried about not having anywhere to live when her grandfather dies."
>
> Jane Nelson, traveled to Africa with the World Help team

She is also HIV positive.

Jane makes regular visits to the local clinic for antiretroviral treatments that could mean the difference between life and death. Before she started receiving her treatments last year, Jane was extremely sick. She couldn't stop coughing. She was so weak she couldn't even get out of bed.

More than just a faceless statistic, Jane's story is a prime example of what's happening all across the globe—entire families being destroyed by AIDS. But despite her fears, Jane has dreams. She has hope.

As I talked with her, I could sense it was difficult

for her to admit she is HIV positive. But by the end of our conversation, she smiled and shared, "I want to do good in school and become a doctor so that someday I can help other sick people."

What unbeatable, unstoppable hope! Her determination in the face of such hopelessness forces me to ask myself: If a little girl living in poverty with a deadly disease can live with such confidence and hope in her future, how can I do less?

Indeed, how can any of us do less? Not only can we *have* hope for the orphans and victims infected with AIDS—we can *give* them hope!

REMOVING THE OBSTACLES

There are many obstacles to helping these children, but perhaps none is more disabling—or easier to change—than the indifferent attitude American Christians demonstrate toward the growing AIDS pandemic. Why haven't more Christ followers joined in the fight against this horrible disease?

Maybe we are just so saturated with photos and reports of the problem that we have become indifferent. But God's Word tells us, *"Finally, all of you, live in harmony with one another; be sympathetic, love as brothers, be compassionate and humble"* (1 Peter 3:8).

The financial resources of the American church

"The best time to plant a tree is 20 years ago; the next best time is today."

African proverb[137]

far outweigh the resources of churches in the regions most affected by HIV/AIDS. These are nations where, in many cases, families earn less than $1 a day, not enough to feed and care for their own children. As a nation that has been blessed with wealth, we must share our resources with those in such great need.

Perhaps we simply think it's someone else's problem. But again, the Bible teaches, *"If anyone says, 'I love God,' yet hates his brother, he is a liar. For anyone who does not love his brother, whom he has seen, cannot love God, whom he has not seen. And he has given us this command: Whoever loves God must also love his brother"* (1 John 4:20-21).

Maybe we think the pandemic of AIDS is just too overwhelming. After all, 42 million[138] currently suffer with the disease, and the number increases every 14 seconds.[139] How can we possibly provide enough ARV drugs to give compassionate care and decrease suffering? There are currently 15 million AIDS orphans.[140] How can we care for them all? We can't! But God is not daunted by the overwhelming statistics of AIDS: *"Jesus looked at them and said, 'With man this is impossible, but with God all things are possible'"* (Matthew 19:26).

The key is not to focus on numbers, but individual

> "Over and over, when I ask God why all of these injustices are allowed to exist in the world, I can feel the Spirit whisper to me, 'You tell me why we allow this to happen. You are my body, my hands, my feet.'"

Shane Claiborne, *The Irresistible Revolution*[141]

lives. How can you and your church change the life of one child? How can you reach out to one orphan with love and compassion?

WHAT CAN ONE PERSON DO?

It's ridiculous to think you or I could alleviate the pain of AIDS all by ourselves. We can't wait to get into the fight until we can do something big. It's the small, deliberate actions that truly make a difference in the lives of others. Too many people are looking for the big payoff. It's all or nothing. But success is not really determined by numbers. Mother Teresa used to say, "We can do no great things, just small things with great love. It is not how much you do, but how much love you put into doing it."[142]

There is much to do. And yes, it may seem overwhelming to try to tackle such a global problem. But we can help change the future for children like Jane whose lives have been turned upside-down by AIDS. We must become voices of hope rather than apathy and despair!

Adoniram Judson was the first Western missionary

to Burma (I know it's Myanmar but many people, including myself, still call it Burma), in the early 1800s.[143] Judson really believed the words of Jesus. He went to Burma primarily to translate the Bible. He hoped against hope that the world could be changed. At the time Burma was nearly 100 percent Buddhist or Animists (people who had never heard about a saving faith in Jesus Christ). He believed the best way he could provide hope was to give them a Bible in their own language.

In the course of Adoniram Judson's ministry, it was at least two years before he even had an opportunity to witness to anyone. It took six years before he saw his first convert. The toll had been high. He buried two of his children. Soon after, civil war broke out and Judson was taken captive by the rebel forces. He was hung upside down by his feet every night, all night long.

Somehow, while he was in prison, he continued to translate the Bible for the people of Burma. Through the course of time, two more of his children died. His wife Nancy got sick and also died. Judson was so distraught at the death of his wife that for two years he had no ministry. He had simply burned out. For six months, he daily meditated at her tomb. He went through clinical depression in an era long before Prozac.

He later remarried, but tragedy continued. He buried two more children and in time, buried his second wife. Yet, he found the strength to continue in his ministry and even married a third time. By his mid-50s, he developed a critical case of tuberculosis. He was advised to travel out to sea, as it was believed the sea air would help. So he journeyed out, never to return. With his wife and remaining children still in Burma, his condition grew worse until he finally died. With no casket and no grave marker, Judson was buried at sea. He was slipped off the side of a boat into the Indian Ocean in total anonymity.

> **"You can throw up your hands in despair [about the sheer numbers of children suffering] . . . or you can roll up your sleeves and get to work."**
>
> **Larry Jones, co-founder, Feed the Children**

By the time of his death there were only about 10 Burmese converts. You may think, "I don't know if it was worth it." After all, in this day we would pull a missionary off the field immediately if they were suffering as he did. But Judson was driven, and so he stayed. We might call it obsessive. In those days they called it compassion.

Even so, his compassion seemed to have brought few results at a very high price. Eventually, he lost all of his financial support from the U.S. and was left high and dry. Was it really worth it?

On my first visit to Burma (Vernon), I met a converted drug addict who was leading a major ministry. He was involved in a church-planting movement, president of a Bible college, directed a drug rehabilitation center with a 90 percent success rate, and helped hundreds of orphaned children and lepers. David Yone Mo was the real deal.

David found out that I collected Bibles from all over the world, so on my last day in Burma, he gave me a gift—a leather-bound Burmese Bible. As I flipped through the pages, I couldn't read a word except for the wonderful inscription David had written on the first page. But the title page was in English. My eyes caught the line, "Translated by the Rev. A. Judson." David asked me if I knew who Adoniram Judson was and I answered quickly, "Oh yes—the very first American missionary." It is unbelievable that Adoniram Judson's translation has withstood the test of time. One hundred seventy-five years later, it is still the translation of preference.

David Yone Mo, with tears in his eyes, looked at me and said, "When Adoniram Judson came to my country there were no Christians. Today, there are more than 6 million Christians in Burma and every one of them without exception can trace their spiritual heritage back to one man . . . an American missionary by the name of Adoniram Judson."

Judson endured because he believed the world could be changed through the power of Jesus Christ and a determined persistent hope that his action—the action of one willing soul—mattered.

Don't lose hope that our world can be changed. When we put our faith and compassion into action, we can change the world, one child at a time, and one family at a time. The key is to get started and persevere.

AGENTS OF HOPE

"If You are willing . . . " Those words lingered in the air. The man who spoke them with his face to the ground in shame was covered with leprosy. In Jesus' day, no one dared touch a leper because the disease was not only disgusting—eating away body parts little by little—it was greatly feared to be highly contagious through contact. This slow, painful killer was also hereditary and thought to be punishment for sin.

Matthew first tells this story, which is echoed by Mark and Luke. Multitudes were following Jesus from the "sermon on the mount" when a leprous man dropped to his knees at the feet of Jesus. The crowd around him surely took a step back and fell silent. The man's humble plea could be heard by all, "Lord, if You are willing, you can make me clean."

By law, Jesus had every right to tell the man to report to the priests and do that which was ceremonially necessary to be cleansed. The Lord could have continued unhindered on His way with a great crowd behind Him. But Jesus doesn't not operate that way and does not expect His children to either.

As the story goes, *"Jesus reached out his hand and touched the man. 'I am willing,' he said. 'Be clean!' Immediately he was cured of his leprosy"* (Matthew 8:3).

Those words "If You are willing," must have

Taking Action

As individuals and as a church body you can make a difference. Following are some steps to impact the AIDS crisis.

- Establish a committee to help launch an awareness campaign in your local church that may extend into your denomination or community.
- Hold an ongoing prayer campaign or periodic prayer vigil for orphans and others impacted by AIDS in sub-Saharan Africa and across the world.
- Devote 1 percent of your personal annual resources to the AIDS fight. Encourage your local church to do the same.
- Designate a committee to research and propose the best plan of action for using the funds.
- Develop a partnership with a local church in sub-Saharan Africa. Adopt that church family as your own and empower them to reach out to their community.
- Be an advocate. Write your representatives to show your concern as a believer.

pierced the heart of Jesus. Of course He was willing!

I ask the same question of you today. Are you willing to touch those who are sick and to feel the compassion of Christ? What if those steeped in poverty, suffering from sickness, and desperate with hunger became more than just a missions effort or

> **"Love without courage and wisdom is sentimentality, as with the ordinary church member. Courage without love and wisdom is foolhardiness, as with the ordinary soldier. Wisdom without love and courage is cowardice, as with the ordinary intellectual, but the one who has love, courage, and wisdom moves the world."**
>
> **Ammon Hennacy, Catholic activist, 1893-1970[144]**

charity campaign? What if they became our brothers and sisters? What if they became our friends and neighbors? What if you experienced their joy and pain on a more personal level, the way Jesus did? What if you reached out to touch them, not just with your hand, but with your heart?

Jesus has called us to do more: *"I tell you the truth, anyone who has faith in me will do what I have been doing. He will do even greater things than these, because I am going to the Father"* (John 14:12). We have a plague among us that surpasses anything the world has ever seen—HIV/AIDS. Where are our greater works?

If we are going to be shapers of the future, we must be agents of hope. We must have faith that Jesus Christ can change people and situations, believing our world can be changed by men and women just like you and me. But to do that, we must not only have faith. We must act on it!

Vincent Donovan, a missionary to the Maasi people of East Africa, discovered that in the Maa language there is no future tense. That gave him great difficulty when it came to translating some of the Bible's promises, like the future return of Christ. Donovan stated, "I think you can say, one of the purposes in evangelizing the Maasi people was to give them a future tense."[145]

And that's our mission for those who have been rendered hopeless by AIDS. We are to give them a future tense—a sense of hope in God's future plans.

Jesus Christ is the source of hope. He gives the most helpless among us, even AIDS orphans like Jane, a reason to fight for life and to hope for a future. Will you be a voice of hope for the children affected by AIDS? If you determine today to take hope to even one child like Jane, you will be doing your part to change the world.

In the past, God's people have shown the light and love of Jesus Christ.

"'For I know the plans I have for you,' declares the LORD, 'plans to prosper you and not to harm you, plans to give you hope and a future.'"

Jeremiah 29:11

When children have been bruised and broken, we have bandaged their wounds.

When children have been hungry, we have fed them.

When children have been alone, we have cared for them.

When children have been hurt, we have comforted them.

Once again, the children need us. They have no one else to turn to.

In South Africa we visited a local public school. More than 200 children welcomed us and shared their stories and poems of hope. Every one of them has been affected by HIV/AIDS in one way or another. One 12-year-old girl stood in front of her classmates and proudly quoted a poem entitled, "I Am the Future." Her name is Unathi, but she speaks for Jane and millions like her. What an incredible glimpse into the heart of these children. It's a cry for help. It's a cry for hope. You and I must answer.

I AM THE FUTURE

"I am the future. I was born into the universe. Not by chance nor by mistake. But by God's grace. I was born into the universe to be loved, to be cared for, and most of all to be nurtured into a priceless soul. So I have a right to be here. Why do you abuse me? Why deny me of my future? Why trample on my innocence? Why betray my trust in you? Don't you know that I am the future? I am the future! Yet evil deeds continue to answer to my emotions. My emotions are vaulting in a stampede. Like a Zulu enemy warrior. Yet your actions have eroded my

sanity, my hope, my future. Don't you know I am the future? I am the future! Future is me and all other children. We are the future!"
—Unathi, age 12, Markman Township, South Africa

HOPE FACTOR

Jane has hope. She now has a sponsor. That means she can go to school and receive the basic necessities like food and clothing because of a special friend who cares for her. And when her grandfather dies, Jane will not have to worry about losing her home. She will be taken care of. "I am so thankful that I get to go to school," she said. When she gets frightened about her illness, Jane said she finds help from God. "I go to church and pray. Then, after praying, I feel much better. I feel much better after hearing the Word of God, too."

There is hope!

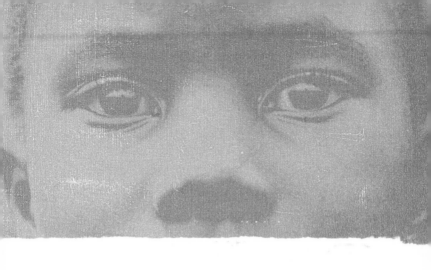

MARTHA

please just help us forget that we are orphans

I met Martha on my first morning in Zambia. She picked us up at our hotel and I immediately liked her. She was energetic, happy and full of passion. We all piled in her van and she drove us into Lusaka. I was anxious to hear about her ministry. I began asking her questions: "What's it like taking care of children who have been infected with HIV/AIDS? Do you have to take any special precautions?"

Martha casually answered, "I have a lot of experience with HIV/AIDS. I am HIV positive." I hope my face didn't show the shock I was feeling inside. "She's HIV positive?" I thought. "This can't be! She looks fine. She's beautiful. She looks so healthy." God was working on my heart and teaching me about the face of AIDS. It can affect anyone, anywhere.

AIDS made Martha an orphan. AIDS made Martha a parent. AIDS made Martha a patient. And AIDS made Martha a fighter.

At 6 years old the little girl from Zambia lost her father. She and her siblings bounced around from home to home as her mother married twice more, seeking a man to care for them. Martha somehow survived and even began attending college. By then, her mother became gravely ill. Martha was told her mother suffered from tuberculosis and pneumonia, but when her mother refused the medicine, Martha confronted her. Sitting by the hospital bed, watching her mother die, Martha learned the truth. The root of her mother's illness was HIV/AIDS. At the time, the medicine to treat her would have cost $1,000 a month. This was more than they could afford. Soon her mother was gone and Martha was left to care for her three brothers and a sister, between ages 2 and 18.

"I had a huge burden. I wanted to keep the family together," Martha said. "I found a job and my major plan was to get married. That was the only way I could see to keep my family together and just stay in a stable environment."

Martha had been dating someone and assumed they would get married. "I figured we were going to get married anyway. And I guess that's why I compromised. I started living with him with the hope that I was going to marry him." But before they were to marry, her boyfriend asked Martha to find someone else to care for her siblings. He didn't want the children. He didn't like the attention and time Martha had to devote to them. But for Martha, that wasn't an option. She was abandoned once again.

Like so many of the people of Africa who have been tested in the most horrible of circumstances, Martha emerged with a spirit of determination. She continued to raise her siblings and pursued an education and a career. It wasn't easy. But Martha had not yet faced her most trying battle.

Eventually, Martha became ill and doctors diagnosed her with malaria and then with tuberculosis. But like her mother, the root of the problem was HIV. Martha's boyfriend had infected her. Doctors prescribed tuberculosis and antiretroviral medication without knowing the combination was deadly. Martha developed a severe rash and lost the use of her legs. She continued to get worse until doctors took her off the ARVs temporarily while she finished the TB doses. She fought her way back to health and her enduring spirit persevered.

Martha told me her viral load is now so low it has been virtually undetectable. "It is a miracle!" she said. "I know God restored my life so that I can serve Him. That gives me a testimony I can share with the kids I deal with. I can make them understand that they are no different if they are HIV positive."

Now, Martha works to give other orphans like herself a fighting chance to live a full and successful life. She helped setup a program in Zambia that provides food, clothing, healthcare, and education to children orphaned and impacted by AIDS.

AIDS does not define Martha's life. She is so much more than that. But being infected has given her a unique and powerful opportunity to reach children that no one else can.

By many on the outside, the people of sub-Saharan Africa are seen as helpless victims without hope. I've heard people say, "What's the point?" or "What can we really do to make a difference? The problem is too great." The people of Africa—I have met them, talked with them, cried with them and stayed with them—are not asking us to solve the problem. They are asking us to give them the tools to fight. They want to be empowered and many have joined this cause to help determined individuals like Martha in the fight of their lives—a fight for lives.

ANTIRETROVIRAL DRUGS (ARVs)

Martha can continue her very effective ministries because she has access to antiretroviral drug therapy. ARV drug treatment has been a life-restoring miracle

The people of Africa—I have met them, talked with them, cried with them and stayed with them—are not asking us to solve the problem. They are asking us to give them the tools to fight this pandemic.

for those infected with HIV and has helped drastically improve their quality of life.[146] These drugs have been proven to extend the lives of people in developed countries, but this wonder drug is not without its own troubles. Costs have prohibited them from being introduced widely to underdeveloped nations.

A year's supply of ARV drugs can exceed $10,000 in the developed world. But in 2003, a coalition of activists persuaded four manufacturers to make ARVs available to developing countries for $140 a year.[147]

Even when the drugs are available, people have a hard time getting to them. They are usually distributed in certain locations, but not everyone has transportation. And when you are sick with HIV/AIDS, you are often too weak to make the journey.

To compound this problem, ARV drugs can be very dangerous. If you take them on an empty stomach or without the right diet, they can kill you. Most of the people who need these drugs cannot afford food most days. And, like with Martha, these drugs used in combination with other drugs can be life threatening.

The good news is that provision of antiretroviral

> "I used to preach at funerals about God giving and God taking away. I don't do that anymore. It is not God's plan that people die at 8 years old. Or 12. Or 30. God gives us the knowledge and skills to prevent or postpone death. Now it's about what people do. We've never seen a disease so vulnerable to the right policies. HIV is not like cancer. If I adopt a combination of prevention approaches and protect the blood supply, the disease will retreat. We know what works. We can defeat AIDS if we do the right things."

Gideon Byamugisha, pastor in Kampala, Uganda[148]

therapy has expanded dramatically in sub-Saharan Africa. In 2002, only 50,000 Africans—1 percent of those who needed ARVs—had them. Today, 28 percent—or 1.34 million people—are getting the treatment.[149] But the bad news is that 5,800 people whose lives could be extended with ARVs are dying of AIDS every day.[150]

ARVs can prolong the lives of those infected with HIV. But they are not a cure. The only real solution is to stop infections and to prevent people from contracting the virus in the first place. And the only truly effective way to do this is through widespread programs that focus on abstinence from sex before marriage and sexual faithfulness after marriage. We must confront the culture!

ABSTINENCE AND FAITHFULNESS

Uganda is one of the success stories in this great saga of survival against HIV/AIDS. President Yoweri Museveni, who favored a nationwide fidelity and abstinence campaign, is known as the most active African head of state in addressing the HIV/AIDS crisis. And the abstinence-first program promoted by the government of Uganda is making progress in the fight.

The infection rate in Uganda, because of abstinence, has fallen from 30 to 10 percent in the last decade.[151] According to studies, Ugandans are taking fewer sexual partners and are practicing fidelity.[152] Between 1991 and 2000, the HIV/AIDS prevalence among pregnant mothers visiting Uganda's prenatal clinics has been cut by two-thirds.[153] Abstinence and continued faithfulness between spouses is the only solution that will ultimately eliminate this disease.

Other countries in Africa have seen their AIDS rates drop as they have used elements of the abstinence and faithfulness message.

Senegal has one of the lowest HIV prevalence rates in sub-Saharan Africa because more people are waiting to have sex and learning about the risks through AIDS education.[154]

In Zimbabwe, both HIV prevalence and incidence has fallen. It appears to be related to a combination of factors, especially reductions in "casual" sex liaisons, AIDS awareness, and relatively extensive health infrastructure. Growing anxiety about AIDS mortality appears to have prompted such behavior changes. In addition, high death rates have contributed considerably to the decline in HIV prevalence.[155]

Rwanda has reduced the HIV-positive proportion of its population from a high of 21 percent in the 1980s to about 3 percent today. Tragically, some of the decrease is attributed to the genocide.[156]

Raising up the new generation of African young people to be abstinent and faithful is the key. While condoms may save lives, they will not end the scourge of AIDS. The ultimate hope is a transformed life by

Some Other Global Initiatives

- International partnerships against AIDS in Africa—a coalition of the United Nations, African governments, civil society organizations and the private sector to curtail the spread of AIDS.
- Global Fund to Fight AIDS, TB and Malaria. www.theglobalfund.org
- International AIDS Vaccine Initiative—the lead agency in the research development, field-testing and approval of a vaccine to prevent HIV/AIDS.
- UNAIDS, the joint United Nations Programme on HIV/AIDS. www.unaids.org
- PEPFAR, the President's Emergency Plan for AIDS Relief, was announced in 2003 by President George W. Bush. It is a five-year, $15 billion program to fund AIDS prevention and treatment in the developing world.[157]

> **"The HIV/AIDS pandemic is the greatest opportunity for the Church to be the Church. It is time for us to be the hands and feet of Jesus to those who need compassion."**
>
> Rick Warren[158]

the Gospel of Jesus Christ. Only He has the power to confront cultures and convince an entire generation to align their behavior to the biblical paradigm of abstinence and faithfulness. Jesus really is the answer!

A MATTER OF FAITH

In the midst of this worldwide catastrophe, there are those in the church community that have shown up as representatives of Christ.

Saddleback Church

Best-selling author and pastor Rick Warren and his wife Kay lead their congregation in Lake Forest, California, in addressing the AIDS crisis through their church's HIV/AIDS initiative. In her testimony, Kay tells of reading an article about Africa and the problem of HIV/AIDS. For days she could not get it out of her mind. She and Rick decided to go to Africa, and it was during this trip that God grabbed their hearts and thrust them into the forefront of this battle. No longer could they see it as someone else's problem. God put this pandemic squarely in front of them, and after wrestling with it they wholeheartedly embraced the challenge God laid before them.

Both Rick and Kay believe that the local church is the one institution to make a lasting difference. Governments, with all of their best intentions, can only attempt to establish laws to regulate the affairs of behavior, or merely provide alternative solutions. However, it is God alone who can change a person's heart as it relates to right thinking leading to right behavior. It is their desire to mobilize 1 billion believers around the world to combat the pandemic of HIV/AIDS. The outgrowth of this is their now widely accepted *PEACE Plan*:

> Plant churches—to address spiritual emptiness (Matt. 16:18)
> Equip leaders—to address corrupt leadership (Mark 3:14)
> Assist the poor—to address extreme poverty (Luke 4:18)
> Care for the sick—to address and care for those suffering from diseases (Matt. 9:35)
> Educate the next generation—to address illiteracy and the lack of education (Matt. 4:23)

The church hosts an annual conference of church leaders, political policymakers, healthcare professionals, nongovernmental organizations (NGOs), relief groups and social workers that explores the problem. I attended their 2006 Global Summit on

AIDS and the Church, with nearly 2,000 delegates, including two U.S. Senators Barack Obama (D-Ill) and Sam Brownback (R-Kan).

Senator Obama's presence caused quite a controversy. And while I do not agree with all of his political views, I do applaud the Warrens for bringing attention to this crisis.

"Let the chorus of those who are suffering be, 'Hallelujah, the church of God has shown up to help!'"

Kay Warren, executive director of Saddleback Church's HIV/AIDS initiative[159]

During the 2006 AIDS Summit, Kay said when God first opened her eyes to the HIV/AIDS pandemic, she was afraid getting involved would tarnish her reputation or Saddleback Church's reputation. Her fears, she realized, came from sinful attitudes. "Jesus was not worried about his reputation ever. He lived boldly. He talked frankly. He hung out with people considered the scum of the earth," Kay said. "I was wrong, and some of you are too."[160]

Willow Creek Community Church

"God will ask us about how our church responded to the greatest humanitarian crisis of our day . . . the AIDS pandemic," said Bill Hybels, senior pastor of Willow Creek Community Church. The Willow Creek Association is fighting the disease by offering financial support to African churches engaged in the battle against AIDS.

The church launched its strategy in 2004, going from no involvement in the global AIDS crisis to becoming actively engaged when Bill's wife Lynne became convinced they should do something. As part of the Year-End Fund Drive in 2004, the Willow Creek congregation raised $600,000 toward the fight against AIDS. The church wanted to encourage and support African churches that were already fighting the war.

One of those partnerships was with Bright Hope International, an organization in Samfya, Zambia, that placed children with loving families and caregivers. In 2005, Willow Creek sent funds for food and school uniforms that allowed Bright Hope to go from caring for 170 orphans and vulnerable children to 500!

Soon everyone in the church wanted to help. Children brought their money. A soccer team held a garage sale and raised $1,500 by selling their toys. As a whole, the children of the church raised $14,000. The middle school ministry raised $2,400 to purchase

> **"As the Church, we must make it unacceptable to look the other way and hope that someone else will solve this problem. We must engage with the passion, resources, and love of God. That is our call to action."**
>
> **Bill Hybels, Willow Creek Community Church**[161]

bikes for caregivers in Africa. Members donated gardening tools, sewing machines, and computers. Companies shared medical supplies and more computers.

The following year, members of the congregation purchased and assembled 11,000 Hope Packs to distribute to every child in Samfya. These packs contained school supplies, toys, hygiene products, a Bible and mosquito netting. The Year-End Fund Drive raised $1.2 million to fight AIDS in Africa and the number of orphans cared for in Samfya increased to 1,000.

"The pandemic is robbing many developing countries of the teachers, farmers and business leaders they need to lift themselves out of poverty. To stop this devastation, we must teach biblically based values, care compassionately for those who are suffering, and share the Good News of salvation."

Franklin Graham, president, Samaritan's Purse[162]

This is an example of what one determined church can do by partnering with local groups and organizations already at work throughout sub-Saharan Africa.

Samaritan's Purse

Through Prescription for Hope projects, Samaritan's Purse is working to unite Christians worldwide in the battle against HIV/AIDS through:

- **Abstinence and Behavior Change Programs for Youth.** Prescription for Hope offers a biblically based curriculum to mobilize, equip and train youth, ages 10-24 to make healthy choices and prevent contraction of HIV.
- **Workshops for Church Leaders.** These workshops teach Christian leaders how to develop positive, nondiscriminatory, culturally relevant approaches to HIV/AIDS in their communities.
- **Support for Mission Hospitals.** Prescription for Hope supports HIV/AIDS prevention education, testing, and treatment programs.

Africa AIDS Initiative

One coalition of churches is working together "for hope and wholeness in the face of AIDS." Mars Hill Bible Church of Grand Rapids, Michigan, Perimeter Church of Atlanta, Georgia, Mariners Church of Irvine, California, and Wooddale Church of Eden Prairie, Minnesota, have formed the Africa AIDS Initiative. The group's vision is to "engage North American churches to join with African churches in collaborative initiatives that transform communities devastated by AIDS."[163]

ROCK STARS, CELEBRITIES AND THE BUSINESS WORLD

While these faith-based organizations and churches have stepped in and rolled up their sleeves to offer Christ's compassion and hope, most Christian artists and congregations have remained strangely distant from the human suffering caused by HIV/AIDS in developing countries.

As Shane Claiborne wrote in *The Irresistible Revolution*, "Perhaps it should not surprise us that Jesus says that if the Christians remain silent, then the rocks will cry out . . . or the rock stars I guess."[164]

Global initiatives have gathered eclectic groups of celebrities and pop stars. But of all the celebrities like Angelina Jolie, Brad Pitt and George Clooney, who are citing the horrors of war, poverty and AIDS on the continent of Africa, possibly none have made a greater impact than Bono, of the Irish rock band U2.

ONE

U2 has performed for several aid projects and helped to organize Live 8. Bono has been part of the ONE Campaign—a movement of more than 2 million people who have signed the ONE Declaration and more than 3 million who are also wearing white bands—both as a show of support for ending extreme poverty and global AIDS.

The campaign, launched by 11 of America's most well-known aid groups (such as Bread for the World, CARE, DATA, Mercy Corps and others), asks

America's leaders to do more to fight the global emergency by giving an extra 1 percent toward providing basic needs like health, education, clean water and food for the world's poorest countries. Currently, the U.S. federal budget allocates only 1.2 percent for International Affairs. Less than half of that is spent on fighting AIDS and poverty around the world.[165]

Bono and his wife Ali Hewson helped launch the EDUN line to use factories on the continent of Africa and other developing countries to encourage business and investment. He has spoken out about the problems of poverty and disease on the continent of Africa before heads of state and policymakers around the world, including the 2006 National Prayer Breakfast held in Washington, D.C.

RED

Bono and Bobby Shriver, chairman of DATA, created RED to raise money and awareness for The Global Fund to Fight AIDS, Tuberculosis and Malaria.

Bono's Remarks at the National Prayer Breakfast

"God may well be with us in our mansions on the hill . . . I hope so. He may well be with us as in all manner of controversial stuff . . . maybe, maybe not. But the one thing we can all agree, all faiths and ideologies, is that God is with the vulnerable and poor.

God is in the slums, in the cardboard boxes where the poor play house . . . God is in the silence of a mother who has infected her child with a virus that will end both their lives . . . God is in the cries heard under the rubble of war . . . God is in the debris of wasted opportunity and lives, and God is with us if we are with them. 'If you remove the yolk from your midst, the pointing of the finger and speaking wickedness, and if you give yourself to the hungry and satisfy the desire of the afflicted, then your light will rise in darkness and your gloom will become like midday and the Lord will continually guide you and satisfy your desire in scorched places.'

It's not a coincidence that in the Scriptures, poverty is mentioned more than 2,100 times. It's not an accident. That's a lot of air time, 2,100 mentions. (You know, the only time Christ is judgmental is on the subject of the poor.) 'As you have done it unto the least of these my brethren, you have done it unto me.' (Matthew 25:40). As I say, good news to the poor. [. . .]

Africans are still dying every day of a preventable, treatable disease, for lack of drugs we can buy at any drugstore. This is not about charity, this is about justice and equality.

Because there's no way we can look at what's happening in Africa and, if we're honest, conclude that deep down, we really accept that Africans are equal to us. Anywhere else in the world, we wouldn't accept it. Look at what happened in Southeast Asia with the Tsunami. One hundred fifty thousand lives lost to that misnomer of all misnomers, "mother nature." In Africa, 150,000 lives are lost every month. A tsunami every month. And it's a completely avoidable catastrophe. [. . .]

History, like God, is watching what we do."

—You can find a transcript of Bono's speech
in Appendix A

The concept is this: the most well-known brands of the world produce RED branded items and a percentage of each product sold is given to The Global Fund to help women and children affected by HIV/AIDS in Africa.

The campaign features partnering companies such as Gap®, American Express®, Converse®, Apple® and more. RED has received much criticism for the millions used in marketing and advertising. I've criticized them myself in the past, saying how that money could better go to help fight AIDS. But the truth, according to founder Shriver, is that this great expense does not come out of money for The Global Fund, but rather from the individual marketing budgets of the companies and partners involved.[166]

You cannot overlook the incredible results. In the project's first nine months, $25 million has gone directly from (RED) partners to The Global Fund, which grants money to healthcare organizations around the world to fight disease. That is more than Australia, Switzerland and China combined contributed to The Global Fund last year.[167]

"I'm optimistic that people's thinking will evolve on the question of health inequity—that people will finally accept that the death of a child in the developing world is just as tragic and worthy of our attention as the death of a child in the rich world."

Bill Gates[168]

With ads in magazines like *Vanity Fair* for these major companies that bring attention to the tragedy with headlines like "Be a good-looking Samaritan"— even the secular world is learning the lessons Christ taught about the importance of being a "Good Samaritan." Suddenly the cause seems trendy.

THE GATES FOUNDATION

The Bill and Melinda Gates Foundation has spent $8 billion on health issues around the world, including AIDS, malaria and tuberculosis. Bill Gates said, "I'm optimistic that people's thinking will evolve on the question of health inequity—that people will finally accept that the death of a child in the developing world is just as tragic and worthy of our attention as the death of a child in the rich world." Melinda Gates said, "I believe the connection happens when you see people as neighbors and not as strangers. The people of Africa are our neighbors."[169]

MADONNA AND MALAWI

While I want to say from the beginning that I do not agree with pop star Madonna's political views, and certainly not her lifestyle, I do admire the compassion she is showing to the children of Malawi.

She established the Raising Malawi organization and began helping to set up Millennium Villages that provide clean water and sanitation infrastructure, schools, maize seed and fertilizer, as well as medical care. She is also working on a documentary about the plight of orphans in Malawi.[170]

According to Madonna, the children need different levels of help. Some need an orphan daycare where they can go for an education and food during the day before they return to their families. Some of the children have no families and need homes and total care. Others need psychological help to deal with their great losses. "No one's addressing what it feels like to lose your parents, and what's going on in the heads and hearts of these kids," Madonna said in a *Vanity Fair* interview. "If they're the future of the country then we need to do something about it."[171]

On her second trip to Malawi last year, Madonna adopted her son David, who was almost two years old at the time and suffering from malaria and pneumonia.[172]

"I believe the connection happens when you see people as neighbors and not as strangers. The people of Africa are our neighbors."

Melinda Gates[173]

She said, "It's difficult to watch people suffer, but it's so hard to watch children suffer. You think, how can I save them all, how can I make their lives better, what is their future?"[174]

I recall the story of a great man of history who worked and partnered with people he disagreed with politically in order to confront the crisis of his day. Many people know the story of William Wilberforce,

"I asked one of the children in Malawi, 'If . . . there's one thing you could say to the world, what would you say?' The boy said, 'Please just help us forget that we're orphans.'"

Madonna[175]

the man who was mightily used to abolish slavery in the British Empire. His story is now being told in a major motion picture—*Amazing Grace*. But what is not well known is the personal cost he faced in his advocacy.

Wilberforce became a Member of Parliament at the young age of 21. He was converted to Christianity in 1784. During the next few years, he struggled with his vocation. What was God's will for him? How could he be both a politician and a devout Christian? In 1787, he wrote in his diary the conviction that God had called him to labor for the abolition of the slave trade. In light of his divine call, as well as the righteousness of the issue, Wilberforce expected a

"This is an emergency—normal rules don't apply. There are no easy good or bad guys. Do you think that an African mother cares if the drugs keeping her child alive are thanks to an iPod or a church plate? Or a Democrat or a Republican? [. . .] So why should we? It can lead to uncomfortable bedfellows, but sometimes less sleep means you are more awake."

Bono[176]

MALAWI AT A GLANCE

Population: 12,884,000
Children orphaned by AIDS: 550,000
Children who have lost at least one
    parent to AIDS: 1 million
People living on less than $1 a day: 42 percent[177]

quick and easy victory. He was sorely mistaken.

Wilberforce began to express in Parliament the claims of slaves in 1787. He became ill, but was able to deliver his first parliamentary speech in 1789. In 1791, the issue came to a vote, but he was defeated. For the next 16 years he persevered in the fight but was repeatedly beaten. It was not until 1804 that Wilberforce won a victory in the (House of) Commons, only to be overthrown in the House of Lords. Finally on February 23, 1807, abolition was secured. The House rose to its feet and broke out in cheers for Wilberforce. He was so overcome with emotion that he sat with his head in his hands, tears streaming down his face.

Amazingly, Wilberforce did not rest long. He knew that while the slave trade was abolished, there were still men in chains. In spite of renewed criticism, threats on his life, and deep-seated prejudice against him, Wilberforce labored until July 26, 1833, when

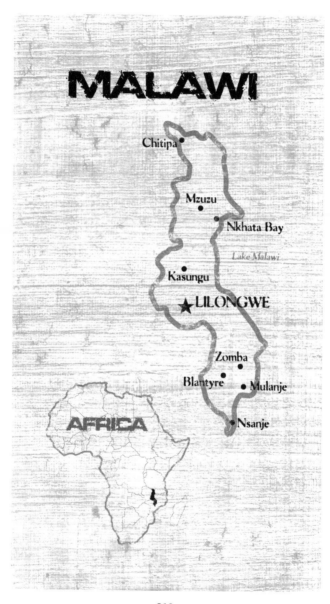

How do we get our arms around 15 million children orphaned by AIDS? It is not impossible. There are 350,000 evangelical churches in America. If every church in America sponsored 42 African AIDS orphans, we literally could save their lives!

the Emancipation Bill passed. Three days later, Wilberforce died.[178]

Just like Wilberforce, other Christians who have come before us have responded to the crisis of their day with love, compassion and great perseverance. Now that it is our turn, what will we do?

I'll never forget the words Martha spoke to me that day. They were so piercing. "Something I have noticed is the attitude toward Africa in general, even Zambia, and the HIV crisis. I think there is a bit of judgmental attitude. I know that because I had it. I judged people that were sick and felt they were maybe careless. And I just never thought that it would happen to me. Now when I look at some of these kids I know that it's not their fault. AIDS can happen to anybody.

"They just need support. And by support, I mean love," Martha said. "That's all I needed to get out of that situation—to know that people would love me the same in spite of what I have been through or what's happened to me. That's all these kids need is to show you love and support them. That's all they need.

That's all."

If we give them help, love and empowerment, they will do the rest.

HOPE FACTOR

Seven-year-old Raziya of Namibia was left alone in the world when both parents died of AIDS. Infected with HIV herself, she was very ill and traumatized. Raziya was taken to live at a children's home but still battled nightmares and bedwetting. She acted out her frustrations by spreading her feces on bathroom walls. But the little girl was transformed after she came to know Jesus. She shared about how "Jesus and an angel visited her" late one night. Raziya said the angel was dressed in white and had "big arms." Jesus had a face that was "shining like the sun" with "a dress down to his feetsies" and holes in his wrists. Raziya thought they were coming to take her but said Jesus told her He was getting medicine for her. What she didn't know was that a donor in the U.S. had pledged money for HIV/AIDS medicines for children at the home who were HIV positive![179]

There is hope!

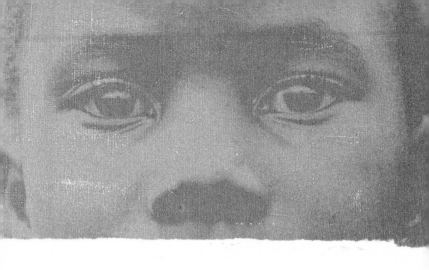

GERTA

villages of hope

Of all the children I met in Africa, Gerta still stands out in my mind. Perhaps it was her near perfect English or her bright smile. It may have been the pink t-shirt she was wearing with the initials G.E.M. displayed prominently. When I asked what this stood for, she replied, "Girls Everywhere Meeting the Savior. At my church, they are teaching us how to live without our parents, how to respect ourselves, and about God."

I'm not exactly sure what it was that made Gerta

so special. Her story was similar to the millions of other children in Africa that have been orphaned by HIV/AIDS. But, despite her troubled past, she had a joy that just seemed to pour out of her, and a hope that can only be found in Jesus Christ.

Gerta's favorite Bible story is the parable of the prodigal son. That sounds odd, considering that at age 18, this sweet girl has probably done very little to identify with this story of forgiveness.

Maybe it's the reunion of family when the wayward son returns home that she enjoys. Or maybe as a child of poverty, she can relate to the desperation of the lost young man who had no home and no food. Possibly, Gerta likes it because the story has a happy ending.

J esus tells this story of a son who leaves home, wastes his entire inheritance and hits "rock bottom." Desperate and hungry, he finds a job feeding pigs. Realizing his foolishness, he returns home, broken and begging for forgiveness. Although his father could have been angry, instead he welcomes him with open arms and has compassion for him.

When facing the overwhelming tragedy of AIDS, children like Gerta, and all of us, could use some hope and encouragement from this story of redemption.

HIV/AIDS has brought Africa to the depths of

despair, just like the prodigal son. Innocent children have been orphaned by it. Spouses have unknowingly contracted it. Millions have died from it and communities and nations are being crippled by it. We are all impacted by this global tragedy and at times, just like with the prodigal son, the situation seems utterly hopeless.

As I walked through villages and stood among grave-filled cemeteries in the different nations on the continent of Africa, I felt the weight of this unprecedented tragedy.

Where could I start? How could I possibly have any impact on such a massive number of children? What do we do? How can we make a difference when the needs and the issues are so mammoth? What's the use? It's hopeless. It's Africa. It's so unfamiliar to anything I've ever experienced. Shouldn't governments with their extensive influence and resources be the ones who fix these problems? Aren't nongovernmental organizations doing everything that can be done? You may be asking yourself these same questions.

So much violence and pain! In a local coffee shop, well-meaning commentators have told me, "That's just what Africans do to each other." Others ask, "How can we help people who do such evil, butchering innocent women and children in Rwanda?" My answer is, "The children are innocent. They are the ones that are suffering the most. These children deserve our help."

The redeeming love of Jesus Christ must be our

The Prodigal Son

There was once a man who had two sons. The younger said to his father, "Father, I want right now what's coming to me."

So the father divided the property between them. It wasn't long before the younger son packed his bags and left for a distant country. There, undisciplined and dissipated, he wasted everything he had. After he had gone through all his money, there was a bad famine all through the country, and he began to hurt. He signed on with a citizen there who assigned him to his fields to slop the pigs. He was so hungry he would have eaten the corncobs in the pig slop, but no one would give him any.

That brought him to his senses. He said, "All those farmhands working for my father sit down to three meals a day and here I am starving to death. I am going back to my father. I'll say to him: Father, I've sinned against God, I've sinned before you; I don't deserve to be called your son. Take me on as a hired hand." He got right up and went home to his father.

When he was still a long way off, his father saw him. His heart pounding, he ran out, embraced him and kissed him. The son started his speech: "Father, I've sinned against God, I've sinned before you; I don't deserve to be called your son ever again."

But the father wasn't listening. He was calling to the servants, "Quick! Bring a clean set of clothes and dress him. Put the family ring on his finger and sandals on his feet. Then get a grain-fed heifer and roast it. We're going to feast! We're going to have a wonderful time! My son is here— given up for dead and now alive! Given up for lost and now found!" And they began to have a wonderful time.

All this time his older son was out in the field. When the day's work was done he came in. As he approached the house, he heard the music and dancing. Calling over one of the houseboys, he asked what was going on. He told him, "Your brother came home. Your father has ordered a feast— barbecued beef!—because he has him home safe and sound."

The older brother stalked off in an angry sulk and refused to join in. His father came out and tried to talk to him but he wouldn't listen. The son said, "Look how many years I've stayed here serving you, never giving you one moment of grief, but have you ever thrown a party for me and my friends? Then this son of yours who has thrown away your money on whores shows up and you go all out with a feast!"

His father said, "Son, you don't understand. You're with me all the time, and everything that is mine is yours— but this is a wonderful time, and we had to celebrate. This brother of yours was dead, and he's alive! He was lost, and he's found!"

Luke 15:11-32, *The Message*

drive. There is hope. But it's going to depend on us!

Even though she lost her parents and lives in great need, Gerta has that hope. "God is there for me," she said. And so was a Christ-like individual who saw her need and put their compassion into action. Through the support of a loving sponsor, Gerta goes to school where she receives an education that will prepare her for the future.

"I want to become a doctor. I want to help others

when they are sick," Gerta said. "Please pray for me. I don't want to be out of the will of God. Anywhere I am going I must have a heart that listens to the will of God." Wise words for us all.

A caring sponsor is helping transform Gerta's life. She has been given a new beginning and hope for a bright future. We all can make a difference. Your church can make a difference. You can make a difference in the life of a child.

PEOPLE JUST LIKE YOU

Here are what some others are doing to provide hope to children all over the world who need it the most.

Benedict Schwartz and the members of Mount Zion United Methodist Church near Baltimore, Maryland, got involved. A few years ago, Benedict felt God calling him to help orphaned children in Africa, and he immediately began talking with friends in his church. In 2002, he started the Children of Zion Village in Namibia, and his church really got excited about it! To date, over 80 people in the church have gone to Namibia in only five years on short-term mission trips. They are making an incredible difference in the lives of 52 children. (In addition, his church has grown from under 300 members to almost 700 during this time.)

SeaCoast Grace Church in Cypress, California, got involved. In 2004, Pastor Doyle Surratt and his family visited the Good Samaritan Children's Home

"If you don't have something in your life that can make your heart pound, that can move you to tears of joy or tears of sorrow in about 30 seconds, then my friend, you are not fully alive. Life is too precious to go on in such a half-awake condition. You can do better. You deserve better. If you don't have such a cause or mission in life, then please take mine!"

Dr. Wes Stafford, *Too Small To Ignore*[180]

and School in Kampala, Uganda, with World Help. Good Samaritan did not have a source of clean water. Doyle, Connie, Cody, and Chelsea saw children hiking down a quarter-mile hill with empty cans to draw water from a dirty spring then trudge back up the hill with the cans full. And because the water was diseased, the 600 Good Samaritan children had regular intestinal problems.

Doyle went home and got his church involved. In just a few days, they provided the funds to build a water system at the home, and for a new water line to connect to the suburban Kampala public water supply. Within weeks, the lives and health of these children were transformed by clean water. Additionally, the city authorities decided to extend Good Samaritan's water line down the long hill to the village areas below. Now literally hundreds of households have clean water. SeaCoast Grace Church reached out and made a difference in the lives of hundreds of orphans and an entire village.

New Life Church in Gahanna, Ohio, got involved. Pastor Steve Benninger and the New Life Church heard the story of the Forgotten Children of Northern Uganda and were moved to do something. The church and a sister organization were able to support two Good Samaritan Children's Centers for a year, helping 100 desperately needy children who were living in refugee camps to get a Christian boarding school education. But that's not where they stopped. A small team from the church went to Uganda and visited the camp where many of these kids had been living. They met the children and went back "pumped up" to get their church friends even more involved. Since then, the New Life family have signed up to sponsor over 60 of these desperately needy Forgotten Children. New Life is committed in a big, long-term way to continue providing hope for formerly hopeless boys and girls.

The Kingdom Partners, a group of businessmen in California, got involved. This group of creative entrepreneurs has organized and hosted a golf tournament for the past four years to help children around the world. They provided the land to build a home in India where 200 children will live. They also provided education and vocational training for over 300 orphans and former child soldiers in Northern Uganda. Most recently, they have raised the funds to care for more than 50 young, poverty-stricken children in different countries from now until they

"I am an AIDS orphan, too."

Francis Michel Kamau, our partner in Zambia, is originally from Kenya. He has worked all over the world for YWAM (Youth With A Mission). He was called home to Kenya when his own mother became ill. "When I got home, I saw a figure lying in bed and I couldn't tell clearly whose features they were. The cheeks were hollow, the eyes were sunken in and the hair had turned a different color. But the closer I got, I realized it was my mother. I had never seen anyone with AIDS before. But I knew, without being told, that it was AIDS."

Francis decided he had to do something. He had to get his mother some help. He picked her up and drove to the nearest hospital. He ran to the entrance of the hospital with his mother in his arms. At the door, one of the staff met him. He looked at Francis's mother, felt for a pulse and shook his head. She was already dead.

"My mother died in my arms. My mother went through the most horrendous, slow and painful death. I felt very lost and alone. It was a deep anguish and pain that I cannot even express. I am an AIDS orphan, too.

"I kept this painful loss a secret for many years, without telling anyone—not even my wife," he said. Now, Francis dedicates his life to helping children like himself who have been orphaned by AIDS. He works in Zambia providing Villages of Hope to give abandoned children a future.

"There is so much potential in these children. God could use these little ones. He could raise up some of these orphans to turn the tide of corruption and hopelessness in this country. They just need someone to encourage them and tell them that God really loves them and He can do awesome things in their lives. I remind them of the story in the Bible of Queen Esther. She was an orphan child. Mordecai raised her up. What

> would have happened if Mordecai was not there when she lost a parent? God elevated this young girl to the highest position of power. In the most critical period—God used her to save thousands of her own people. So how do we know that these orphans may not bring salvation and deliverance to this country?"

finish their high school education.

The Kingdom Partners—just a few men very busy with their families and professional lives who also happen to like golf—are using their creativity and their pastime to provide hope to hundreds of children around the world and to involve others as well.

Amy, Rachel, April, Nancy, Hannah, Ben, Jaime and many others in our office at World Help got involved. They sponsor children. They each help one or two children on a monthly basis, many through a deduction from their paycheck. Their regular giving provides hope for their very special child. They have the photos of their children prominently displayed at home and at their desks and pray for them daily. Our staff is making an incredible impact in children's lives. They're doing something to make a difference.

Frank and Mary Kathryn Moomaw got involved. When Frank, a retired construction executive, joined the World Help Board of Directors, he and his wife saw the need to help children in

Uganda who had been orphaned by AIDS and other diseases. They decided to provide the resources to build an additional floor at the Good Samaritan Children's Home in Kampala. Now, 120 more children have a place to live with wonderful caregivers and good schooling. Frank and Mary Kathryn found a way to help that resonated with them and have made an incredible impact in many young lives.

Their monthly giving provides for food, clothing, education, and hope for their very special child. Our staff is making an incredible impact in children's lives.

Tony Foglio and Sonrise Community Church in Santee, California, will be involved. Tony and his wonderful congregation have caught the vision for helping children who are affected by HIV/AIDS. They want to build a Village of Hope to provide a home and a loving environment for almost 50 children whose parents have died of AIDS. Tony is making it simple for the church by challenging them to each commit $10 per week for two years to provide for this village. It will be so exciting as they work together to see this vision become a reality.

WHAT ARE YOU WILLING TO DO?

Wes Stafford says, "If you don't have something in your life that can make your heart pound, that can move you to tears of joy or tears of sorrow in about 30 seconds, then my friend, you are not fully alive. Life is too precious to go on in such a half-awake condition. You can do better. You deserve better. If you don't have such a cause or mission in life, then please take mine!"[181]

I echo his words . . . take my cause . . . take my mission . . . join us!

I want to challenge and invite you to do something today to help the children of Africa affected by HIV/AIDS. The immense and incredibly complex problems facing children in the developing world, as a result of HIV/AIDS, civil wars, poverty, and genocide are truly overwhelming. We certainly don't think we can understand the whole problem—let alone solve it. But God understands it. He can solve it. And God has shown World Help the role He wants us to play.

• Be a Voice of Hope—Child Sponsorships

God has given World Help the incredible opportunity to help people in the U.S. connect with needy children around the world. Our Child Sponsorship Program has provided over 22,000 sponsorships for children in 22 countries. But we also want to reach out to these children affected by HIV/AIDS.

We have waiting lists of thousands of orphans and needy children. We want to pair these special children with thousands of individuals and families who can provide support for them.

A monthly sponsorship provides food, clothing, education, and most importantly, a Christ-centered focus in a child's life.

We are not just helping a child whose life has been impacted by HIV/AIDS. We are investing in the future—future Christian leaders, future teachers, nurses, businessmen, church planters and pastors. It's an investment that will be multiplied a generation from now. It gives a young boy or girl hope—in the words of Jeremiah, *"For I know the plans I have for you," declares the Lord, "plans to prosper you and not to harm you, plans to give you hope and a future"* (Jeremiah 29:11).

• **Villages of Hope**

We are committed to a proven effective strategy to provide help and hope for children whose extended families simply cannot care for them by establishing "Villages of Hope" throughout sub-Saharan Africa. Each Village of Hope will care for as many as 48 orphaned children in four small, family-like Homes of Hope. The homes will be headed by a widowed caregiver, or a young couple who are Christ followers and are committed to helping these children. Each 900-square-foot, three-bedroom home will provide a place of love, care and security for 12 children.

The Villages of Hope will not be "compounds" that remove children from their culture and community. Located in or near existing villages, they will utilize local schools and medical clinic facilities to provide education and healthcare for the children. The Village of Hope will be tightly integrated with its local neighbors, helping not only the 48 children in the homes but also many others in the greater community.

Some of these villages will be situated on farms, which provide tremendous resources for additional training and long-term self-sufficiency. The farms will be a fertile "training ground" for both the children as they grow older and many other teenagers and young adults in the villages and nearby communities—as they provide vocational skills, employment opportunities, and create microbusiness startups for many unemployed young men and women.

The young children who live in these Homes of Hope will be bathed in God's love as they grow. They will see His love in action every day. These Homes give the children the opportunity to grow up within their culture, rather than removed from it. God and their caregivers will be preparing them to make a difference in their village or community a generation from now.

In addition to the homes, each Village of Hope

"I am here . . . I want to do something for these children, because I know God has a purpose and a plan for each and every one of these lives to bless not only Zambia and Africa, but who knows, the world!"

Francis Michel Kamau, Village of Hope partner

will also have a multi-purpose "community center" building that will be used for training, continuing education, and as a church.

The first Village of Hope, located just north of Lusaka, Zambia, is now occupied by incredibly needy orphaned children between the ages of 3 and 6. Our long-term hope and desire is to reproduce this proven model all over Africa. Our vision is to see hundreds of villages and homes, caring for thousands of children whose lives have been turned upside-down by HIV/AIDS. Can you imagine?

• **Centers of Hope**

Our partners in Uganda are making a huge difference in the lives of children in the most needy parts of this country. In addition to the Glory of Virginity Movement (GLOVIMO) program and the Good Samaritan Children's Centers that have been established in Northern Uganda, we want to provide "Centers of Hope" in the rural "bush" areas in the rest of the country. These centers—with leadership provided by local churches and staffed by healthcare and social workers and vocational training instructors—will provide a holistic outreach to the nearby bush villages and communities. Each center will:

- provide immediate help to hundreds of orphans and needy children
- allow believers to take a lead role in providing programs that benefit the

children, as well as AIDS awareness and Christ-centered health education training classes. These programs stress the value of abstinence before marriage and faithfulness after marriage

- have a small medical clinic to provide basic care to treat malaria, respiratory infections, wounds and injuries, helping thousands of people who've never had access to medical care
- include a vocational training program and an athletic field that will almost immediately and naturally make the center a "regular meeting place" for the children in the area

Our vision is that these Centers of Hope will transform entire groups of villages by providing education, training, medical attention, and most importantly—hope!

Our goal is to provide Centers of Hope throughout sub-Saharan Africa. The first of these centers is located in an area about 30 miles from Kampala, Uganda. The property is strategically located on a hillside in the middle of five separate villages. The medical clinic is up and running, and helping over 300 patients every month.

A CALL TO ACTION

I want to issue a personal challenge: Get involved.

Every child in the area has an opportunity to hear the Gospel, develop a personal relationship with Jesus, and grow up with wise mentors who disciple them as they get older.

Get off the sidelines. These problems are not just "African problems." They are everyone's problems. As Mama Gladys told us, "they are all our children."

It is not right to simply pray and ask God to do something when He has already given us the ability and power to do it. These children certainly need prayer, but they also need action—your action!

In the words of contemporary theologian Jack Riemer:

> "We cannot merely pray to You,
> O God, to end war;
> For we know that You have made
> the world in a way that man must
> find his own path to peace within
> himself and with his neighbor.
>
> We cannot merely pray to You, O
> God, to end starvation;
> For You have already given us the
> resources with which to feed the
> entire world, if we would only use
> them wisely.

We cannot merely pray to You,
O God, to root out prejudice;
For You have already given us eyes
with which to see the good in
all men, if we would only use them
rightly.

We cannot merely pray to You,
O God, to end despair;
For You have already given us
the power to clear away slums and
to give hope, if we would only use
our power justly.

We cannot merely pray to You,
O God, to end disease;
For You have already given us great
minds with which to search out
cures and healing, if we would only
use them constructively.

Therefore, we pray to You instead,
O God,
For strength, determination, and
willpower, to do instead of just pray,
to become instead of merely
to wish."[182]

Will you get involved? Will you take action? Will

you join us? Be a Voice of Hope. Be an Agent of Hope. Here's what you can do:

PRAY. Pray some more. Pray continuously without ceasing. Pray for the millions of children that have been orphaned by AIDS. Pray for the children whose lives have been torn apart and who have been robbed of their childhoods by war and genocide. Pray that God would break your heart and let you see the suffering children in Africa through His eyes. Pray that He would show you where to get involved, how to get connected, how to make a difference and how to provide hope.

READ AND STUDY. Educate yourself. The fact that you're reading this book means you're starting to get involved. There is so much more you can read, learn and study. To help you, we have included a resource guide at the end of this book.

BE A VOICE OF HOPE. Give hope to a child, or to several children, through our Child Sponsorship Program. Show the Children of Hope video to a group of your friends and family. Commit to find 10 or even 100 other people who will sponsor a child.

BECOME AN AGENT OF HOPE. Share this book with others and get them involved. Tell them about the problem of children who have been orphaned or affected by HIV/AIDS and help them learn how they can become involved as well.

PROVIDE VILLAGES OF HOPE. You can provide an entire Village of Hope to help 48 orphans out of helplessness, or a single Home of Hope to reach twelve children orphaned by AIDS. You can make an incredible difference in so many lives by giving them hope right now!

GO WITH US TO AFRICA. Get your hands dirty. Go to Zambia, Uganda, Rwanda or South Africa. Experience the culture. Let your heart be broken as you come face-to-face with the needs and see the plight of these children. Then let your heart be encouraged as you see how God can use you to bring help and hope!

THE IMPACT OF YOUR INVOLVEMENT

I have two questions that keep coming to mind—"Have I clearly and passionately told their story? Have I shown the urgency?"

This book is about the children of Africa, children affected in some way by poverty, wars, genocide and HIV/AIDS. You have heard their stories and you have heard their cries for help. And, you will determine how this story ends for children like Gerta, Nozake, Phila-Sande, Josianne and others. The future of these children is very much dependent upon our action—or lack of action.

" Either you decide to leave people to die, or you decide to do something about it."

Jeffrey Sachs, *The End of Poverty*[183]

I pray these children have touched your heart and inspired you to action. But, the question is—have they changed you?

Vision is seeing the invisible and making it visible. Can you see the possibilities as you allow God to work through you to reach out to these children? I can.

I can see the child you sponsor in Rwanda becoming an incredible teacher or evangelist.

I can see the 12 children you provide with a Home of Hope in Zambia becoming effective farmers, nurses, or community leaders.

I can see the impact God will make in your life as you take that very first short-term mission trip. I can see it changing your life in ways you never imagined.

I can see the friends and family you share with and challenge to get involved accomplishing far bigger things than any of us ever thought possible.

I can see an entire generation of children orphaned by AIDS being taught the importance of abstinence before marriage and faithfulness in marriage. AIDS can be stopped—one child at a time!

Please, get involved. Be touched. Be inspired. Be changed. Together, we can make a difference and give hope to millions of children affected by AIDS—the Children of Hope.

HOPE FACTOR

You are the hope for these children. Hope is a word of action—a word of power. It's the spark for change, the fuel for endurance and the warmth of success. Hope gives the struggling something to cling to and the determined something to build upon. Hope gives assurance, peace and strength for tomorrow. It promises a fresh start and a better future.

Prayerfully consider what you can do to get involved. But don't stop there! Don't forget about these children. Don't let your heart grow cold. Commit today to become a voice of hope—an agent of hope. God can use you to change the world!

You hold the power to give hope today! You can show these children a promise-filled future. And in doing so, they will also be your hope. They will give you a passion, purpose and meaning. They will change your world. They will be your Children of Hope.

There is hope!

Appendix A

BONO:

Mr. President, First Lady, King Abdullah, other heads of state, members of Congress, distinguished guests . . .

[. . .]

If you're wondering what I'm doing here, at a prayer breakfast, well, so am I. I'm certainly not here as a man of the cloth, unless that cloth is leather. It's certainly not because I'm a rock star. Which leaves one possible explanation: I'm here because I've got a messianic complex.

Yes, it's true. And for anyone who knows me, it's hardly a revelation.

Well, I'm the first to admit that there's something unnatural . . . something unseemly . . . about rock stars mounting the pulpit and preaching at presidents, and then disappearing to their villas in the South of France. Talk about a fish out of water. [. . .]

It's very humbling and I will try to keep my

homily brief. But be warned—I'm Irish.

I'd like to talk about the laws of man. [. . .] And I'd like to talk about higher laws. It would be great to assume that the one serves the other; that the laws of man serve these higher laws . . . but of course, they don't always. And I presume that, in a sense, is why you're here.

I presume the reason for this gathering is that all of us here—Muslims, Jews, Christians—all are searching our souls for how to better serve our family, our community, our nation, our God.

I know I am. Searching, I mean. And that, I suppose, is what led me here, too.

Yes, it's odd, having a rock star here—but maybe it's odder for me than for you. You see, I avoided religious people most of my life. Maybe it had something to do with having a father who was Protestant and a mother who was Catholic in a country where the line between the two was, quite literally, a battle line. Where the line between church and state was . . . well, a little blurry, and hard to see.

I remember how my mother would bring us to chapel on Sundays . . . and my father used to wait outside. One of the things that I picked up from my father and my mother was the sense that religion often gets in the way of God.

For me, at least, it got in the way. Seeing what religious people, in the name of God, did to my native land . . . and in this country, seeing God's secondhand car salesmen on the cable TV channels, offering indulgences for cash . . . in fact, all over the world, seeing the self-righteousness roll down like a mighty stream from certain corners of the religious establishment . . .

I must confess, I changed the channel. I wanted my MTV.

Even though I was a believer.

Perhaps because I was a believer.

I was cynical . . . not about God, but about God's politics. [. . .]

Then, in 1997, a couple of eccentric, septuagenarian British Christians went and ruined my shtick—my reproachfulness. They did it by describing the Millennium, the year 2000, as a Jubilee year, as an opportunity to cancel the chronic debts of the world's poorest people. They had the audacity to renew the Lord's call—and were joined by Pope John Paul II, who, from an Irish half-Catholic's point of view, may have had a more direct line to the Almighty.

"Jubilee"—why "Jubilee"?

What was this year of Jubilee, this year of our Lord's favor?

I'd always read the Scriptures, even the obscure stuff. There it was in Leviticus (25:35) . . .

'If your brother becomes poor,' the Scriptures say, 'and cannot maintain himself . . . you shall maintain him . . . You shall not lend him your money at interest, not give him your food for profit.'

It is such an important idea, Jubilee, that Jesus begins his ministry with this. Jesus is a young man, he's met with the rabbis, impressed everyone, people are talking. The elders say, he's a clever guy, this Jesus, but he hasn't done much . . . yet. He hasn't spoken in public before . . .

When he does, his first words are from Isaiah: "The Spirit of the Lord is upon me," he says, "because He has anointed me to preach good news to the poor." And Jesus proclaims the year of the Lord's favor, the year of Jubilee (Luke 4:18).

What he was really talking about was an era of grace—and we're still in it.

So fast-forward 2,000 years. That same thought, grace, was made incarnate—in a movement of all kinds of people. It wasn't a bless-me club . . . it wasn't a holy huddle. These religious guys were willing to get out in the streets, get their boots dirty, wave the placards, follow their convictions with actions . . . making it really hard for people like me to keep their distance. It was amazing. I almost started to like these church people.

But then my cynicism got another helping hand.

It was what Colin Powell, a five-star general, called the greatest W.M.D. of them all: a tiny little virus called AIDS. And the religious community, in large part, missed it. The ones that didn't miss it could only see it as divine retribution for bad behavior. Even on children . . . even when the fastest growing group of HIV infections were married, faithful women.

Aha, there they go again! I thought to myself . . . judgmentalism is back!

But in truth, I was wrong again. The church was slow but the church got busy on this the leprosy of our age.

Love was on the move.

Mercy was on the move.

God was on the move.

Moving people of all kinds to work with others they had never met, never would have cared to meet . . . conservative church groups hanging out with spokesmen for the gay community, all singing off the same hymn sheet on AIDS . . . soccer moms and quarterbacks . . . hip-hop stars and country stars . . . This is what happens when God gets on the move: crazy stuff happens!

Popes were seen wearing sunglasses!

Jesse Helms was seen with a ghetto blaster!

Crazy stuff. Evidence of the spirit.

It was breathtaking. Literally. It stopped the world in its tracks.

When churches started demonstrating on debt, governments listened—and acted. When churches starting organizing, petitioning, and even that most unholy of acts today, God forbid, lobbying on AIDS and global health, governments listened—and acted.

I'm here today in all humility to say: you changed minds; you changed policy; you changed the world.

Look, whatever thoughts you have about God, who He is or if He exists, most will agree that if there is a God, He has a special place for the poor. In fact, the poor are where God lives.

Check Judaism. Check Islam. Check pretty much anyone.

I mean, God may well be with us in our mansions on the hill . . . I hope so. He may well be with us as in all manner of controversial stuff . . . maybe, maybe not . . . But the one thing we can all agree, all faiths and ideologies, is that God is with the vulnerable and poor.

God is in the slums, in the cardboard boxes where the poor play house . . . God is in the silence of a mother who has infected her child with a virus that will end both their lives . . . God is in the cries heard under the rubble of war . . . God is in the debris of wasted opportunity and lives, and God is with us if we are with them. "If you remove the yolk from your midst, the pointing of the finger and speaking wickedness, and if you give yourself to the hungry and satisfy the desire of the afflicted, then your light will rise in darkness and your gloom with become like midday and the Lord will continually guide you and satisfy your desire in scorched places."

It's not a coincidence that in the Scriptures, poverty is mentioned more than 2,100 times. It's not an accident. That's a lot of airtime, 2,100 mentions. (You know, the only time Christ is judgmental is on the subject of the poor.) "As you have done it unto the least of these my brethren, you have done it unto me" (Matthew 25:40). As I say, good news to the poor.

Here's some good news for the President. After 9-11 we were told America would have no time for the world's poor. America would be taken up with its own problems of safety. And it's true these are dangerous times, but America has not drawn the blinds and double-locked the doors.

In fact, you have doubled aid to Africa. You have tripled funding for global health. Mr. President, your emergency plan for AIDS relief and support for the Global Fund—you and Congress—have put 700,000 people onto life-saving antiretroviral drugs and provided 8 million bed nets to protect children from malaria.

Outstanding human achievements. Counter-intuitive. Historic. Be very, very proud.

But here's the bad news. From charity to justice, the good news is yet to come. There's much more to do. There's a gigantic chasm between the scale of the emergency and the scale of the response.

And finally, it's not about charity after all, is it? It's about justice.

Let me repeat that: It's not about charity, it's about justice.

And that's too bad.

Because you're good at charity. Americans, like the Irish, are good at it. We like to give, and we give a lot, even those who can't afford it.

But justice is a higher standard. Africa makes a fool of our idea of justice; it makes a farce of our idea of equality. It mocks our pieties, it doubts our concern, it questions our commitment.

6,500 Africans are still dying every day of a preventable, treatable disease, for lack of drugs we can buy at any drugstore. This is not about charity, this is about Justice and Equality.

Because there's no way we can look at what's happening in Africa and, if we're honest, conclude that deep down, we really accept that Africans are equal to us. Anywhere else in the world, we wouldn't accept it. Look at what happened in Southeast Asia with the Tsunami. 150,000 lives lost to that misnomer of all misnomers, "mother nature." In Africa, 150,000 lives are lost every month. A tsunami every month. And it's a completely avoidable catastrophe.

It's annoying but justice and equality are mates. Aren't they? Justice always wants to hang out with equality. And equality is a real pain.

You know, think of those Jewish sheep-herders going to meet the Pharaoh, mud on their shoes, and the Pharaoh says, "Equal?" A preposterous idea: rich and poor are equal? And they say, "Yeah, 'equal,' that's what it says here in this book. We're all made in the image of God."

And eventually the Pharaoh says, "OK, I can accept that. I can accept the Jews—but not the blacks."

"Not the women. Not the gays. Not the Irish. No way, man."

So on we go with our journey of equality.

On we go in the pursuit of justice.

We hear that call in the ONE Campaign, a growing movement of more than 2 million Americans . . . left and right together . . . united in the belief that where you live should no longer determine whether you live.

[...]

Preventing the poorest of the poor from selling their products while we sing the virtues of the free market ... that's a justice issue. Holding children to ransom for the debts of their grandparents ... that's a justice issue. Withholding life-saving medicines out of deference to the Office of Patents ... that's a justice issue.

And while the law is what we say it is, God is not silent on the subject.

That's why I say there's the law of the land ... and then there is a higher standard. There's the law of the land, and we can hire experts to write them so they benefit us, so the laws say it's OK to protect our agriculture but it's not OK for African farmers to do the same, to earn a living?

As the laws of man are written, that's what they say.

God will not accept that.

Mine won't, at least. Will yours?

[pause]

I close this morning on ... very ... thin ... ice.

This is a dangerous idea I've put on the table: my God vs. your God, their God vs. our God ... vs. no

God. It is very easy, in these times, to see religion as a force for division rather than unity.

And this is a town—Washington—that knows something of division.

But the reason I am here, and the reason I keep coming back to Washington, is because this is a town that is proving it can come together on behalf of what the Scriptures call the least of these.

This is not a Republican idea. It is not a Democratic idea. It is not even, with all due respect, an American idea. Nor [is it] unique to any one faith.

"Do to others as you would have them do to you" (Luke 6:30). Jesus says that.

"Righteousness is this: that one should . . . give away wealth out of love for Him to the near of kin and the orphans and the needy and the wayfarer and the beggars and for the emancipation of the captives" (2.177). The Koran says that.

Thus sayeth the Lord: "Bring the homeless poor into the house, when you see the naked, cover him, then your light will break out like the dawn and your recovery will speedily spring forth, then your Lord will be your rear guard." The Jewish scripture says that. Isaiah 58 again.

That is a powerful incentive: "The Lord will watch your back." Sounds like a good deal to me, right now.

A number of years ago, I met a wise man who changed my life. In countless ways, large and small, I was always seeking the Lord's blessing. I was saying, you know, I have a new song, look after it . . . I have a family, please look after them . . . I have this crazy idea . . .

And this wise man said: stop.

He said, stop asking God to bless what you're doing.

Get involved in what God is doing—because it's already blessed.

Well, God, as I said, is with the poor. That, I believe, is what God is doing.

And that is what He's calling us to do.

I was amazed when I first got to this country and I learned how much some churchgoers tithe. Up to 10 percent of the family budget. Well, how does that compare to the federal budget, the budget for the entire American family? How much of that goes to the poorest people in the world? Less than 1 percent.

[. . .]

I want to suggest to you today that you see the flow of effective foreign assistance as tithing . . . Which, to be truly meaningful, will mean an additional 1 percent of the federal budget tithed to the poor.

What is 1 percent?

One percent is not merely a number on a balance sheet.

One percent is the girl in Africa who gets to go to school, thanks to you. One percent is the AIDS patient who gets her medicine, thanks to you. One percent is the African entrepreneur who can start a small family business thanks to you. One percent is not redecorating presidential palaces or money flowing down a rat hole. This 1 percent is digging waterholes to provide clean water.

One percent is a new partnership with Africa, not paternalism towards Africa, where increased assistance flows toward improved governance and initiatives with proven track records and away from boondoggles and white elephants of every description.

America gives less than 1 percent now. We're asking for an extra 1 percent to change the world . . . to transform millions of lives—but not just that and I say this to the military men now—to transform the way that they see us.

One percent is national security, enlightened economic self-interest, and a better safer world rolled into one. Sounds to me that in this town of deals and compromises, 1 percent is the best bargain around.

These goals—clean water for all, school for every child, medicine for the afflicted, an end to extreme and senseless poverty—these are not just any goals; they are the Millennium Development goals, which this country supports. And they are more than that. They are the Beatitudes for a Globalised World.

Now, I'm very lucky. I don't have to sit on any budget committees. And I certainly don't have to sit where you do, Mr. President. I don't have to make the tough choices.

But I can tell you this:

To give 1 percent more is right. It's smart. And it's blessed.

There is a continent—Africa—being consumed by flames.

I truly believe that when the history books are written, our age will be remembered for three things: the war on terror, the digital revolution, and what we did—or did not do—to put the fire out in Africa.

History, like God, is watching what we do.

Thank you. Thank you, America, and God bless you all.

SOURCE:
http://www.usatoday.com/news/washington/
2006-02-02-bono-transcript_x.htm

Appendix B

Resources for further study

BOOKS:
28: stories of AIDS in africa. Stephanie Nolen. Walker & Company, 2007.

A Guide to Acting on AIDS: Understanding the Global AIDS Pandemic and Responding Through Faith and Action. Jyl Hall, Laura Barton, Michaela Dodd, James Pedrick, and Jackie Yoshimura (editors). Authentic Media, 2006.

Black Death: AIDS in Africa. Susan Hunter. Palgrave MacMillan, 2004.

Children Affected by HIV/AIDS: Compassionate Care. Phyllis Kilbourn (editor). MARC, 2002.

The Hope Factor: Engaging the Church in the HIV/AIDS Crisis. Tetsunao Yamamori, David Dageforde, and Tina Bruner (editors). Authentic Media, 2004.

There Is No Me Without You: One Woman's Odyssey to Rescue Africa's Children. Melissa Fay Greene. Bloomsbury USA, 2007.

The Skeptic's Guide to the Global AIDS Crisis. Dale Hanson Bourke. Authentic Media, 2006.

The Son of God Is Dancing: A Message of Hope. Adrian Plass and Bridget Plass. Authentic Media, 2005.

The Truth About AIDS—and a practical Christian response. Dr. Patrick Dixon. ACET International Alliance in partnership with Operation Mobilisation, 2004.

DVDs:
A Closer Walk. Robert Bilheimer, 2002.

Dear Frances. Chronicle Project, 2005.

Hope and Action. Willow Creek Community Church, 2006.

Hope Positive. Crossroads International and 95 Theses Entertainment.

The Age of AIDS. PBS/FRONTLINE production, 2006.

WEBSITES:

Global Fund to Fight AIDS, TB, and Malaria: www.theglobalfund.org

Global Health Council: www.globalhealth.org

International Union Against TB and Lung Diseases: www.iuatld.org

Massive Effort Campaign: www.massiveeffort.org

Roll Back Malaria: www.rbm.org

The ONE Campaign: www.one.org

UNAIDS: www.unaids.org

UNDP: www.undp.org

World Bank: www.worldbank.org

World Health Organization: www.who.org

World Help: www.worldhelp.net

Endnotes

INTRODUCTION

1   Mark DeMoss, *The Little Red Book of Wisdom*, Nashville, Tennessee: Thomas Nelson, Inc., 2007, 1.

2   DeMoss 6.

3   Stephen Covey, *The 7 Habits of Highly Effective People*, 1989, 97.

4   "Worldwide HIV & AIDS Statistics Commentary," avert.org, http://www.avert.org/worlstatinfo.htm.

DINDI

5   "Worldwide HIV & AIDS Statistics Commentary," avert.org, http://www.avert.org/worlstatinfo.htm.

6   Stephanie Nolen, *28: stories of AIDS in africa*, New York: Walker Publishing Company, Inc., 2007, front flap.

7   Susan Hunter, *Black Death:AIDS in Africa*, New York: Palgrave MacMillan, 2003, 22.

8   Tetsunao Yamamori, David Dageforde, Tina Bruner eds., *The Hope Factor: Engaging the Church in the HIV/AIDS Crisis*, Waynesboro, Georgia: Authentic Media, World Vision Press, 2003, 186.

9   "Fighting AIDS," The Global Fund, http://www.theglobalfund.org/en/about/aids.

10   Chambers Dictionary, Larousse plc: 1996, 347.

11   "Zambia Statistics," UNICEF, http://www.unicef.org/infobycountry/zambia_statistics.html, AVERT, "AIDS ORPHANS," http://www.avert.org/aidsorphans.htm.

12   Hunter v.

13   Charlayne Hunter-Gault, *New News Out of Africa:*

Uncovering Africa's Renaissance, New York: Oxford
University Press, Inc. 2006, 122.

14   Phyllis Kilbourn ed., *Children Affected by HIV/AIDS:
      Compassionate Care*, Monrovia,
      California: MARC Books, 2002, 146.

15   Andrea Bakke, Corean Bakke, *Time to Talk in Church
      about HIV and AIDS*, Acme, Washington: Bakken Books,
      2004, 63.

16   Dale Hanson Bourke, *The Skeptic's Guide to the Global
      AIDS Crisis*, Waynesboro, Georgia:
      Authentic Media, 2004, 5.

17   Ibid.

18   Hunter 22.

19   *Black Death: AIDS in Africa*,
      www.themiddleages.com/plague.html.

20   Maggie Fox, "AIDS will create 40 million orphans - U.S.
      report," Reuters News Media, Inc., 19 Nov. 1997,
      http://www.aegis.com/news/re/1997/RE971112.html.

21   Julia Post, " '14 Million Dreams': The Compelling Stories
      of 5 Children Orphaned by AIDS in Africa," 24 Nov.
      2003, Global Health Council,
      http://www.globalhealth.org/news/article/3792.

22   Kilbourn 9.

23   Melissa Fay Greene, *There is No Me Without You*, New
      York: Bloomsbury USA, 2006, 20-21.

24   Greene 22.

25   Greene 316.

26   Kilbourn 22.

27   Ibid.

28   Greene 164.

29   Kilbourn 18.

30   Kilbourn 66.

31   "Chambers" 766.

32   Yamamori 19.

33   UN News Centre website, "UNICEF appeals on behalf of
      Zimbabwe's children, now with fastest rise in mortality,"

18 March 2005, http://www.un.org/apps/news/
story.asp?NewsID=13703&Cr=aids&Cr1.

34   Yamamori 228.

35   Ibid.

36   Yamamori 188.

37   Yamamori 252.

GLADYS

38   Nelson Mandela, as quoted in Jennifer
      Crwys-Williams ed., *In the Words of Nelson
      Mandela*, Johannesburg, South Africa: Penguin Books,
      2004, 21.

39   GLOVIMO (The Glory of Virginity Movement —
      Uganda) Report, 1.

40   "An Investment of Mercy for Children Affected by
      HIV/AIDS," Compassion International pamphlet, 10.

41   Laurie Goering, "A light in the darkness: Her family
      decimated by AIDS, Hlengiwe Leocardia Mchunu is
      taking on South Africa's culture of denial about the
      disease," 26 Nov. 2006, *Chicago Tribune*, 2006, 11.

42   "South Africa Statistics," UNICEF,
      http://www.unicef.org/infobycountry/
      southafrica_statistics.html, "HIV & AIDS in South
      Africa," AVERT,
      http://www.avert.org/aidssouthafrica.htm.

43   "An Investment of Mercy for Children Affected by
      HIV/AIDS" 10.

44   Nolen 65.

45   Sharon LaFraniere, "New AIDS Cases in Africa
      Outpace Gains," 6 June 2007, *The New York Times*.

46   Yamamori 261.

47   Dr. Wess Stafford, *Too Small To Ignore: Why
      Children Are the Next Big Thing*, Colorado Springs,
      Colorado: WaterBrook Press, 2005, 175.

48   Bourke 14.

49   Nelson Mandela, as quoted in Jennifer Crwys-Williams

ed., *In the Words of Nelson Mandela*, Johannesburg,
South Africa: Penguin Books, 2004, 22.

50   Bourke 28.

51   UNAIDS, http://www.unaids.org/en/Regions_
      Countries/Regions/SubSaharanAfrica.asp
      28: stories of AIDS in africa, page 11.

52   Emma Guest, *Children of AIDS: Africa's Orphan Crisis*,
      Sterling: Pluto Press, 2001, 66.

NOZAKE

53   Yamamori 186.

54   Yamamori xi.

55   Hunter 23.

56   Greene 276-277.

57   Hunter-Gault 41.

58   Hunter-Gault 122.

59   Hunter 24.

60   Hunter, page v, preface.

61   Dr. Ingrid Woolard., "An overview of poverty and in-
      equality in South Africa, 3.

62   United Nations, "UNAIDS Fact Sheet; HIV/AIDS and
      Food Security," Geneva: UNAIDS,
      September, 2003.

63   Lori Bollinger and John Stover, *The Economic
      Impact of AIDS*, The Futures Group Int., 1999, 5.

64   United Nations, "UNAIDS Fact Sheet; HIV/AIDS and
      Food Security," Geneva: UNAIDS,
      September, 2003.

65   Hunter 23.

66   Yamamori 190.

67   Dr. Ingrid Woolard, "An Overview of Poverty and
      Inequality in South Africa," July 2002, 3.

68   Bourke 3.

69   Laurie Goering, "Why AIDS deaths keep rising in South
      Africa," 26 Nov. 2006, *Chicago Tribune*, 2006, 11.

THANDO

70   Hunter 28.

71   Hunter 28.

72   Hunter 29.

73   Shane Claiborne, *The Irresistible Revolution: Living as an Ordinary Radical*, Grand Rapids, Michigan: Zondervan, 2006, 51.

74   Claiborne 133.

75   Stafford 3.

76   The World Health Report 2006, WHO.

77   Stafford 175.

78   The World Health Report 2006, WHO.

79   Bono, "Guest Editor's Letter: Message 2U," *Vanity Fair*, July 2007, 32.

80   Nina Munk, "Jeffrey Sachs's $200 Billion Dream," *Vanity Fair*, July 2007, 141.

81   www.amref.org/index.asp?PageID=50&PiaID=1

82   "On the Cover," *Vanity Fair*, July 2007, 52.

83   Munk 141.

84   Claiborne 157.

85   Munk 142.

86   Terri Cooney, Kathleen Schwartz, *Adopted for the Kingdom*, Churchville, Maryland: Children of Zion, Inc., 2005, 155.

87   Hunter 28.

88   Ibid.

89   Dr. Patrick Dixon, *The Truth About AIDS*, Kingsway 1994, updated 2002, http://www.globalchange.com/ttaa/ttaa%207.htm.

90   Munk 143.

91   Claiborne 164-165.

92   Claiborne 151.

93   Claiborne 153.

94   Claiborne 164.

95   Claiborne 151.

96   Speech by Bono for February 2006 National Prayer

Breakfast, Washington, D.C. "Transcript: Bono
remarks at the National Prayer Breakfast."
http://www.usatoday.com/news/washington/2006-02-
02-bono-transcript_x.htm, Feb. 2, 2006.

97   Hunter 29.

98   Bono, February 2006 National Prayer Breakfast.

GRACE

99   "Uganda Statistics," UNICEF, http://www.unicef.org/
      infobycountry/uganda_statistics.html.

100   Priya Abraham, "One Dark Night," *World*, 12 Nov. 2005,
      16 Mar. 2006 <http://www.worldmag.com/arti-
      cles/11258>.

101   "Understanding the War," Uganda Conflict Action Net-
      work report published as part of the Congressional
      Human Rights Caucus, Washington, D.C., 8-9 Mar. 2006.

102   J. Carter Johnson, "Deliver Us from Kony,"
      Christianity Today, January 2006, 31.

103   Jennifer Brea, http://worldnews.about.com/od/africa/tp/
      africacivilwar.htm.

104   Johnson 32.

105   "Northern Uganda: Humanitarian Response to Crisis Still
      a Failure," *Refugees International Bulletin*, 27 Feb. 2006.

106   "Northern Uganda: Humanitarian Response."

107   "Real Voices: Uganda's 'night commuters' live in shadow
      of fear," *AlertNet*, 11 Aug. 2005, 30 Apr. 2006.

108   Vernon Brewer, *The Forgotten Children: Hungry.
      Hopeless. Running for their lives.*, Forest, VA: World Help,
      2006, 73-79.

JOSIANNE

109   "Rwanda: facts and figures," UNICEF Information by
      country,
      http://www.unicef.org/infobycountry/23867.html.

110   Central Intelligence Agency, "The World Factbook,
      Rwanda" https://www.cia.gov/library/publications/

the-world-factbook/geos/rw.html.

111   BBC online report, "Rwanda: How the genocide happened,"
       http://news.bbc.co.uk/1/hi/world/africa/1288230.stm.

112   "Rwanda Statistics," UNICEF,
       http://www.unicef.org/infobycountry/rwanda_
       statistics.html, CIA The World Factbook
       https://www.cia.gov/library/publications/the-world-
       factbook/geos/rw.html.

113   Wendy Whitworth ed., *We Survived: Genocide in
       Rwanda*, "Historical Background," Nottinghamshire, UK:
       Quill Press, 2006, 9.

114   Whitworth 9.

115   Whitworth 11.

116   BBC, http://news.bbc.co.uk/1/hi/world/
       africa/1288230.stm.

117   Whitworth 11.

118   "Rwanda: facts and figures," UNICEF
       http://www.unicef.org/infobycountry/23867.html.

119   UNICEF, Rwanda facts and figures,
       http://www.unicef.org/infobycountry/23867.html.

120   Kigali Memorial Centre, Rwanda.

121   "Rwanda: facts and figures," UNICEF,
       http://www.unicef.org/infobycountry/23867.html.

122   Stafford 35.

NILDO

123   Charles Swindoll, *Come Before Winter*, Living Books,
       1988.

124   Ibid.

125   Dr. Paul Brand, Philip Yancey, *Fearfully and Wonderfully
       Made*, Zondervan, 1987.

126   Yamamori 247.

127   Claiborne 89.

128   Rodney Stark, *The Rise of Christianity: A Sociologist
       Reconsiders History*, Princeton University Press, 1996.

129   Max Lucado's book, *The Cure for the Common Life*,
       Nashville, Tennessee: W Publishing Group, 2006.

130   Oswald Chambers, *My Utmost for His Highest Journal
       Edition – Selections for a Year*, Barbour Publishing, 1995,
       Dec. 2 entry.

131   Charles Swindoll, *Compassion: Showing Care in a
       Careless World*, Waco, Texas: Word Books, 1984.

132   Claiborne 102.

133   Yamamori 228.

134   Claiborne 127.

135   Yamamori 228-229.

136   Yamamori 254.

JANE

137   Yamamori 303.

138   "At a Glance Statistics," AIDS.org,
       http://www.aids.org.au/aids-statistics.htm.

139   "Global HIV infecting youth: From the U.N. State of the
       World Population Report," http://www.aids.org.au/news-
       41.htm.

140   "Worldwide HIV & AIDS Statistics Commentary,"
       http://www.avert.org/worlstatinfo.htm.

141   Claiborne 65.

142   Claiborne 78.

143   http://www.wholesomewords.org/biography/biorpjud-
       son.html.

144   Claiborne.

145   Vincent J. Donovan, *Christianity Rediscovered*, Orbis
       Books, 2003.

MARTHA

146   Yamamori 4.

147   "The Lazarus Effect," *Vanity Fair*, July 2007, 158.

148   Nolen 268.

149   "The Lazarus Effect" 160.

150   "The Lazarus Effect" 160.

151 Yamamori xi.

152 Ibid.

153 Yamamori 21.

154 Yamamori 74.

155 "UNAIDS/World Health Organization Sub-Saharan Africa fact sheet," www.unaids.org.

156 "The Lazarus Effect" 222.

157 "Individual websites as noted, *28: stories of AIDS in africa*.

158 "HIV/AIDS: What Your Church Can Do," Saddleback Church DVD.

159 Ibid.

160 Manda Gibson, "At Global Summit, Churches challenged to take the lead," http://www.purposedriven.com/en-US/HIVAIDSCommunity/GlobalConference/2006Conference/Churches_challenged_to_take_lead.htm.

161 "The Courageous Leadership Award for The Hope of the World," WCA News, Issue 1, 2007.

162 Franklin Graham, "Prescription for Hope: A Christian Response to HIV/AIDS," Samaritan's Purse DVD, 2006.

163 Yamamori 265.

164 Claiborne 17-18.

165 http://www.one.org/faq#What%20is%20ONE.

166 "The Lazarus Effect" 222.

167 *Vanity Fair* 32.

168 *Vanity Fair* 54.

169 Ibid.

170 Punch Hutton, "Raising Malawi: Madonna lends a hand," *Vanity Fair*, 80.

171 "Saving Malawi's Children," *Vanity Fair* (VF.COM), 5 June 2007, http://www.vanityfair.com/politics/features/2007/07/kim200707.

172 Hutton 80.

173 *Vanity Fair* 54.

174 "Saving Malawi's Children."

175 *Vanity Fair* 54.

176   "On the Cover," *Vanity Fair,* July 2007, 52.
177   "Malawi Statistics," UNICEF,
       http://www.unicef.org/infobycountry/malawi_
       statistics.html, Punch Hutton, "Raising Malawi:
       Madonna lends a hand," Vanity Fair, 80.
178   Yamamori 238-239.
179   *Adopted for the Kingdom,* page 153-154.

GERTA
180   Stafford 256.
181   Stafford 256.
182   Harold S. Kushner, *When Bad Things Happen to Good
       People,* Avon Publishing, reissue edition, 1983, 130-131.
183   *Vanity Fair* 142.

About the Authors

VERNON BREWER is the founder and president of World Help, a nonprofit, nondenominational Christian organization that was founded to meet the spiritual and physical needs of hurting people around the world.

Vernon is also author of *The Forgotten Children: Hungry. Hopeless. Running for their lives.* and *Why? Answers to Weather the Storms of Life.*

His incredible life experiences, combined with his passion for the unreached peoples of the world, make him an energetic and compassionate leader. His strategic thinking and emphasis on partnership have breathed new life into the mission world and provided innovative ways to partner together and accomplish more for the Kingdom of God.

"I wish that all Christians could see the world as I have seen it . . . to actually see firsthand the masses of hurting people, the hungry and orphaned children, the displaced families, the lepers, the poor, as well as experience the smells and sounds. But even more than that, I wish for you to see the world through the eyes of God."

Vernon has conducted international evangelistic campaigns and rallies in over 50 foreign countries worldwide, as well as numerous leadership training conferences in Uganda, China, India, Nepal, Burma,

Romania and Russia. In addition, he has personally taken over 4,000 people to the mission field. He has led over 500 local church evangelistic rallies, and has lectured on 30 college and university campuses. He has spoken to over 1 million teenagers in public high school assembly programs and is a frequent speaker at camps and conferences.

Vernon lives with his wife Patty and his son Josh in Forest, Virginia. He has three married daughters and four grandsons.

NOEL BREWER YEATTS has a heart and passion for missions. As the daughter of an evangelist and missions leader, she started traveling abroad at the age of 11. At this young age she was exposed to the needs of the world and her life was forever changed.

Wherever Noel traveled, she was impacted most by the needs of the children. A young orphan boy on the streets of Rio de Janeiro taught Noel that God can use each of us to make a difference and that lives can be changed . . . one child at a time.

Noel is the founder of World Help's Child Sponsorship Program that has provided over 22,000 sponsorships for children in need around the world. She has traveled extensively and has ministered in over 12 countries including Uganda, Zambia, Rwanda, South Africa, Russia, Brazil, China, and India.

Noel has been on staff with World Help since inception and has served as Director of Child Sponsorship and Director of Humanitarian Aid. She currently serves as a board member and Director of Communications for World Help.

Noel is a graduate of Liberty University where she studied Government and Speech with an emphasis in Foreign Affairs. She lives in Lynchburg, Virginia, with her husband Patrick and their two sons Riley and Bentley.

About World Help

World Help is a nonprofit, nondenominational Christian organization that exists to fulfill the Great Commission and the Great Commandment through partnering, training, helping and serving, especially in the unreached areas of the world.

Since our founding in 1991, World Help has touched 60 countries through our ministries. We have seen and responded to the spiritual and humanitarian needs of people groups around the world.

We do this through four pillars of ministry: Humanitarian aid, child sponsorship, Bible distribution and church planting.

HUMANITARIAN AID. God loves and cares about suffering people. And if we share God's heart, we must see the world through His eyes—a world in need.

Hunger, war, famine, disease and natural disaster create a worldwide climate of suffering that most of us cannot begin to comprehend.

World Help has seen firsthand the incredible suffering and hardships that people around the world endure every day of their lives. It is our desire to meet the physical needs of hurting people around the world and in so doing, earn the right to be heard!

With the support of individuals, churches, organizations and medical facilities, World Help has shipped over 132 ocean-going containers and distributed critically needed humanitarian aid worldwide at an estimated value of $76 million.

CHILD SPONSORSHIP. Millions of people around the world suffer hardship, hunger and disease. But those who suffer the most are the children. They endure unimaginable living conditions on a daily basis without any hope of a better future.

In the face of these great needs one can feel overwhelmed. World Help's Child Sponsorship Program was born out of the desire to "change the world . . . one child at a time." World Help has provided over 24,000 sponsorships for children in desperate need around the world. Sponsors provide the basic necessities a child needs . . . food, clothing, medical attention and educational opportunities. Most importantly, these children receive the message that God loves them and has a special plan for their lives.

BIBLE DISTRIBUTION. World Help has witnessed an immense hunger for God's Word all around the world. Thousands risk their lives every day for the sake of the Gospel. Pastors, church leaders, Christians of all nationalities plead with us to provide them with Bibles—and we can help them!

The Bible is the most powerful tool God has given us to reach the souls of lost people throughout our world. It is the most important resource we can place in any believer's hand.

World Help was founded on fulfilling this most basic and desperate need. Since inception, we have printed and distributed more than 8 million Bibles, New Testaments and other pieces of Christian literature to places where they are needed the most.

CHURCH PLANTING. "Go and make disciples of all

nations" was the last command Jesus gave His disciples. Jesus did not command us to do the impossible, nor did He command us to go to the ends of the earth with His Gospel if He did not expect us to obey. However, today there are still entire groups of people who have never heard of Jesus Christ.

Church-planting movements are the key to evangelizing the least-reached peoples of the world. Utilizing national church planters, effective church-planting movements penetrate entire people groups with the Gospel. It is the vision of World Help to help plant indigenous, reproducing churches where no churches currently exist. To date, God has allowed our partners to plant over 38,000 churches in the unreached areas of the world.

> *"Thousands have partnered with World Help and God has allowed us to see countless lives miraculously changed, thousands of churches planted in places where there were none, children receiving help and hope through sponsorships, and millions of Bibles provided to those who have never seen a Bible, much less owned one. Together, we are committed to sharing Christ's love, His hope and peace with the unreached people of this world."*

—Vernon Brewer

World Help is also committed to faithful stewardship of funds entrusted to us by donors. We promise to use your gifts wisely and effectively in Christ's name and provide information, a network of international contacts, and financial and ministry accountability for each mission project in which we participate. World Help strives to keep overhead costs to a minimum using only 7% for the administration of our various projects. All gifts designated for specific projects are used as designated. To ensure our financial accountability to you, World Help is a member of the Evangelical Council for Financial Accountability (ECFA) and an annual financial report is readily available for anyone requesting a copy.

For more information about World Help and our outreaches and programs and to learn how you can join us in carrying out the Great Commission and the Great Commandment, visit our website at **www.worldhelp.net**.

What Others Are Saying

"Like artists with their brushes, the authors use stories to paint graphic depictions of the world's forgotten children—the AIDS orphans. These heart-breaking scenarios not only lift the veil on the tragic realities of this global pandemic, but strikes deep in one's heart the conviction that only a compassionate response as mandated and modeled to us by Christ will restore the "hope and future" promised them by their heavenly Father."

PHYLLIS KILBOURN
Director, Crisis Care Training International
Author, *Children affected by HIV/AIDS: Compassionate Care*

"Vernon Brewer's newest book is a wake-up call to any of us who think we understand the AIDS crisis in Africa. Together with his daughter Noel, Vernon cuts through the stigma and ignorance surrounding the disease to lay bare the reality of millions of children growing up without parents—and without hope. This is the worst human catastrophe the world has ever faced. We must do something. While the enormity of the situation is overwhelming, we can each make a difference in the lives of these children for generations to come. Here's how."

DOYLE SURRATT
Senior Pastor, SeaCoast Grace Church, Cypress, CA

"*Children of Hope* is the most compelling book ever written on ministering to the 15 million children who have been orphaned by HIV/AIDS. Vernon and Noel write from broken hearts, tear-filled eyes and, yet, with incredible hope, compassion and love. Don't miss this book. It will inform your mind, move your heart and stretch your faith."

DR. ED HINDSON
Assistant Chancellor, Liberty University

"In *Children of Hope* Vernon raises AIDS compassion as he tells the compelling stories of AIDS orphans while presenting the facts about the disease and the plight of its orphans. The message of the book is clear. Christians have the opportunity in this generation to become the agents of hope."

LUIS BUSH
International Facilitator, Transform World Connections

"There is no group in the world that I know of that is doing more to help underprivileged children than Vernon Brewer and World Help. Through their efforts, there is finally some hope on the horizon for the 15 million children who have been orphaned as a result of the HIV/AIDS crisis in Africa. This book chronicles the tragic story of many of these children. It also shows how we can make a difference in these children's lives."

JONATHAN FALWELL
Pastor, Thomas Road Baptist Church, Lynchburg, VA

"Vernon Brewer's *Children of Hope* demonstrates why we can no longer stereotype the HIV/AIDS epidemic. To ignore it is the equivalent of having ignored the Holocaust. This book has radically changed my view of HIV/AIDS and the need for God's people to care about its innocent victims."

TONY FOGLIO
Founding Pastor, Sonrise Community Church,
Santee, CA

"Having been involved with HIV/AIDS for over 20 years, I cannot think of a greater challenge and opportunity for the church in the 21st century. Every person of faith ought to care and be involved."

DR. ED DOBSON
Pastor Emeritus, Calvary Church,
Grand Rapids, MI

"Vernon Brewer and Noel Yeatts have written a book that cannot be ignored, and cannot be put down. With vivid imagery, moving stories and passionate pens, they have written the definitive call to action for Christians. Do not just read this book—devour it. It is biblically sound, thoroughly evangelical, and emotionally stirring."

DR. ERGUN MEHMET CANER
President, Liberty Theological Seminary
Professor of Theology, History and Apologetics

"As a pastor for more than 40 years, I have always taught that only two things last forever; God's Word and people. It is in these priorities that our time, resources, and energies ought to be spent. I am also fully aware of the HIV/AIDS pandemic in our world, and believe the Church, more than ever before, must get involved. Scripture says to, "...look after widows and orphans in their distress..." My good friend Vernon Brewer and World Help are doing their part to fulfill this mandate by making a difference in the lives of children."

DR. DAVID JEREMIAH
Senior Pastor, Shadow Mountain Community Church,
San Diego, CA

"No one understands the heartbreaking realities around our globe better than World Help. No one tells the stories with more passion and conviction than Vernon Brewer. In our lives, there are some voices we cannot afford to ignore. Vernon's voice is one, because he speaks on behalf of millions around the world that are crying out for our help. Listen to those voices as you read this book."

DANIEL HENDERSON
President, Strategic Renewal International

"Half of the world's population is youth and children. This book, *Children of Hope*, will help people see the children who have been orphaned by HIV/AIDS. May God use this book to awaken the awareness of the Christian world to this dilemma, so we can pray . . . give financially . . . and help in any way we can."

DR. ELMER TOWNS
Vice President, Liberty University
Dean, School of Religion

Be a Voice of Hope.
Sponsor a child today!

Millions of children around the world suffer hardship, hunger and disease. They endure unimaginable living conditions without hope for a better future. Most will never be told that Jesus loves and cares for them.

God can use you to make a difference.

As a World Help child sponsor, you can ignite a spark of hope in the life of a child. You can become a special friend to a child who desperately needs someone to care.

Just $30 a month provides the basic necessities a child needs. Along with food, clothing, educational opportunities and medical attention comes the message that God loves them, and that a very special friend loves them too.

If you would like to sponsor a child, we will send you a packet containing your child's photograph and personal description. We will also show you how to develop a special relationship with your child by corresponding one-on-one with them. You will stay informed of your child's progress through periodic updates.

Make an eternal difference in the life of a child by becoming a child sponsor!

**For more information, call 1-800-541-6691
or log onto our website at www.worldhelp.net.**

*Somewhere in the world a child awaits your compassionate response.
Please say "yes" today and give help and hope to a needy child.*

STAY INFORMED!

Keep updated on all that you are accomplishing around the world through the many outreaches of World Help ...

... by logging onto www.worldhelp.net!

Our high-impact website will inform and inspire you! Take a look for yourself and you will be amazed at the colorful presentations, the heart-touching stories and testimonies, the incredible photography, and the exciting online videos. This user-friendly site will take you through the many ministries and outreaches of World Help, as we share our vision and background, and let you know of opportunities that will allow you to step into the mission field from your own home. Check us out!

... by signing up for regular email reports!

Sign up today to receive regular updates and information about the outreaches and ministry opportunities of World Help via email. It's so quick and easy. Just go online at www.worldhelp.net and click on the "World Help Emails" icon. You will receive regular reports on the impact we are making around the world together in Christ's name.

Get your FREE
HOPE MAGAZINE
subscription!

This magazine will keep you updated on all our global work together. You will see vivid, 4-color photos of the very people you are impacting and read incredible testimonies of how God is using World Help through the prayers and support of friends like you.

This quality news publication will also address the latest issues, reports and needs from around the world and show how World Help is involved.

To view the latest issues of HOPE Magazine or sign up for your FREE subscription, go to www.worldhelp.net and click on "HOPE Magazine" under the "Get Involved" listing.

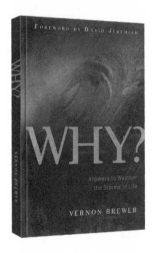

NOTES

NOTES

NOTES

NOTES

NOTES

NOTES

NOTES

NOTES

NOTES

NOTES

NOTES

NOTES